Collins

The Shanghai Maths Project

For the English National Curriculum

一课一练

Homework Guide 1

Author: Paul Broadbent

Homework Guide Series Editor: Amanda Simpson

Practice Books Series Editor: Professor Lianghuo Fan

Contents

Chapter 5 Consolidation and enhancement

Chapter 6 Numbers up to 100

Chapter 7 Introduction to time (I)

Chapter 8 Let's practise geometry

1.1 Let's begin

Count and match objects to 10

1. Join pairs that go together.

2. Count and then match.

Finding pairs

Go on a hunt around the house to find things that go together, for example a pair of socks or a pen and paper.

Show your child one object and ask them to find the partner. You could hide it somewhere! Talk about why they go together.

1.2 Let's sort (1)

Sort objects by 2 or more criteria

1. Colour the shells to show two sets.

2. Circle the odd one out in each group.

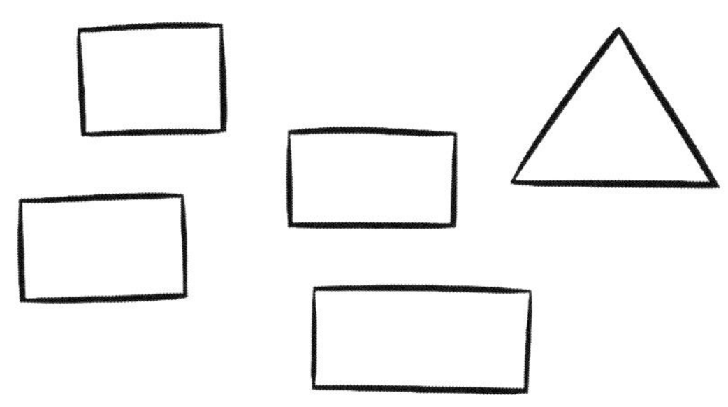

Odd one out

Put a set of seven or eight identical items into a box. Add one that is different and give the box a shake. Ask your child to find the odd one out. Ask: *Why is it the odd one out?* Take turns so they have a go at making a set with an odd one out and explaining why.

You will need:
buttons, coins or counters of different sizes, colours and shapes.

1.3 Let's sort (2)

Sort objects in different ways

1. Circle each set of objects that are the same in some way.

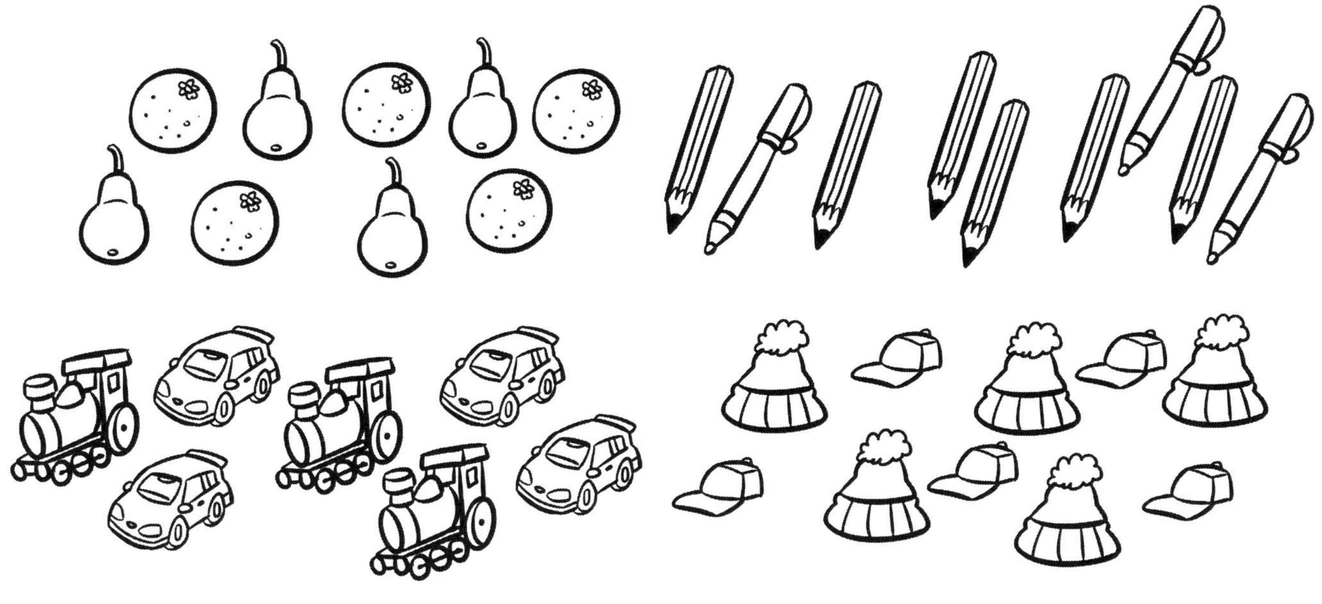

2. Colour the bears to make a set. Choose a way to sort them.

Sorting out

Ask your child to take a handful of different buttons and then sort them into two groups. To help with the sort you can use a large piece of blank paper with a line drawn down the centre to show two sorting areas. Ask how they sorted the buttons and what is the same and what is different about each set.

You will need:
buttons, coins or counters of different sizes, colours and shapes.

1.4 Let's count (1)

Count and recognise numerals to 10

1. Join each number to the matching picture.

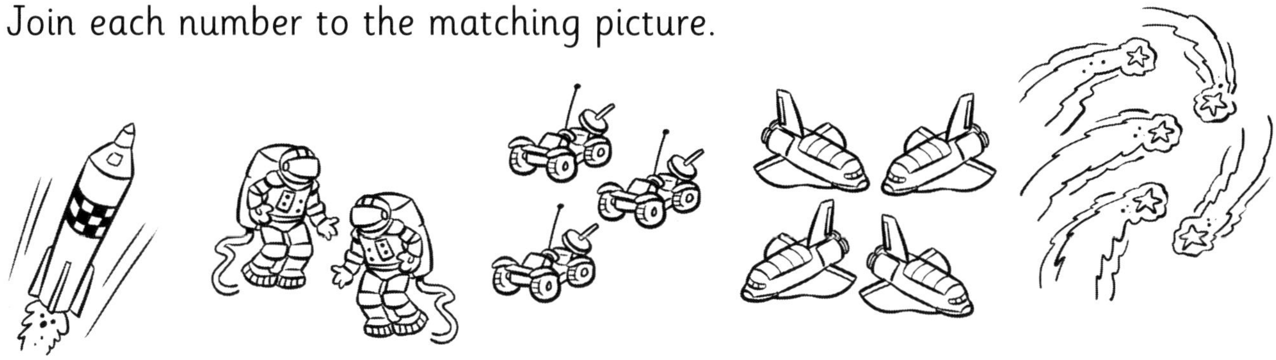

1 2 3 4 5 6 7 8 9 10

2. Write the numbers to match each word.

□	□	□	□	□
one	two	three	four	five
●	●●	●●●	●●●●	●●●●●

□	□	□	□	□
six	seven	eight	nine	ten
●●●●● ●	●●●●● ●●	●●●●● ●●●	●●●●● ●●●●	●●●●● ●●●●●

Number labels

Give your child squares of paper for them to write numbers on. They choose a number and write it on a square and then try to match it by counting pegs or small toys. Ask them to leave the pegs in a group with the labels so they can check their count again later.

You will need:
paper, pegs or small toys.

1.5 Let's count (2)

Count and write numbers to 10

1. Count each group. Write the numbers.

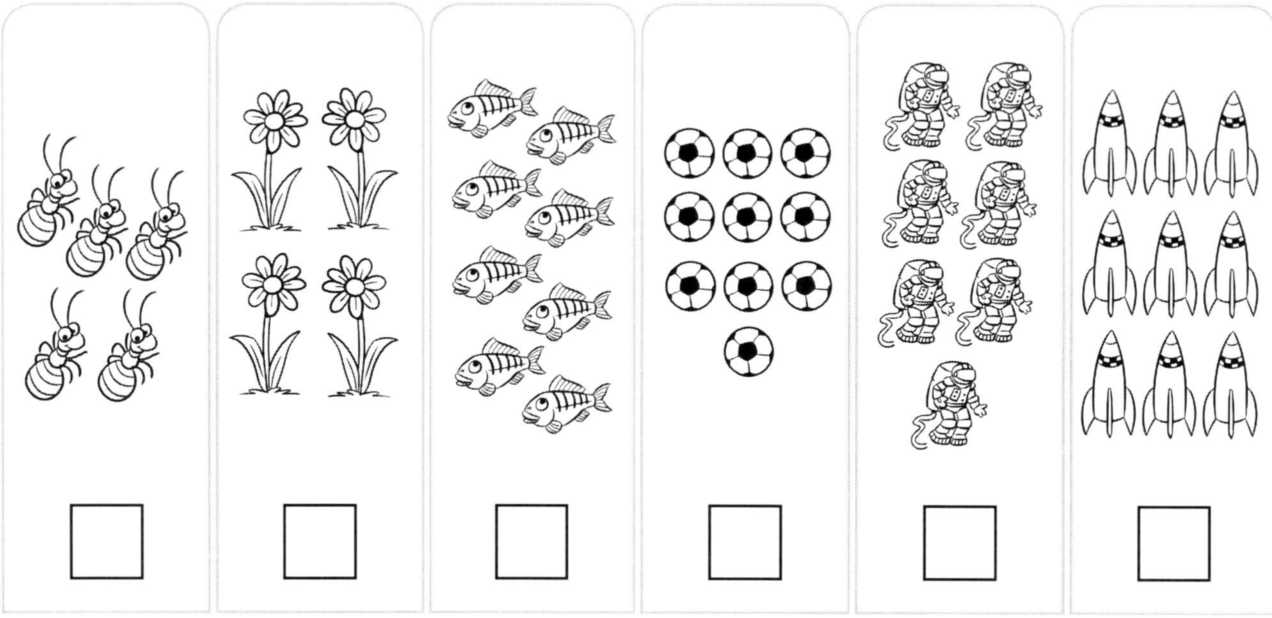

2. Count and colour the dots to match. Write the numbers.

		six	6

Counting out

As you put away household objects, such as clothing or kitchen items, take the opportunity to count aloud with your child. Make deliberate mistakes so that they correct you and then ask them to reinforce the correct number by counting out again.

1.6 Let's count (3)

Sort and count shapes

1. Count how many of each shape.

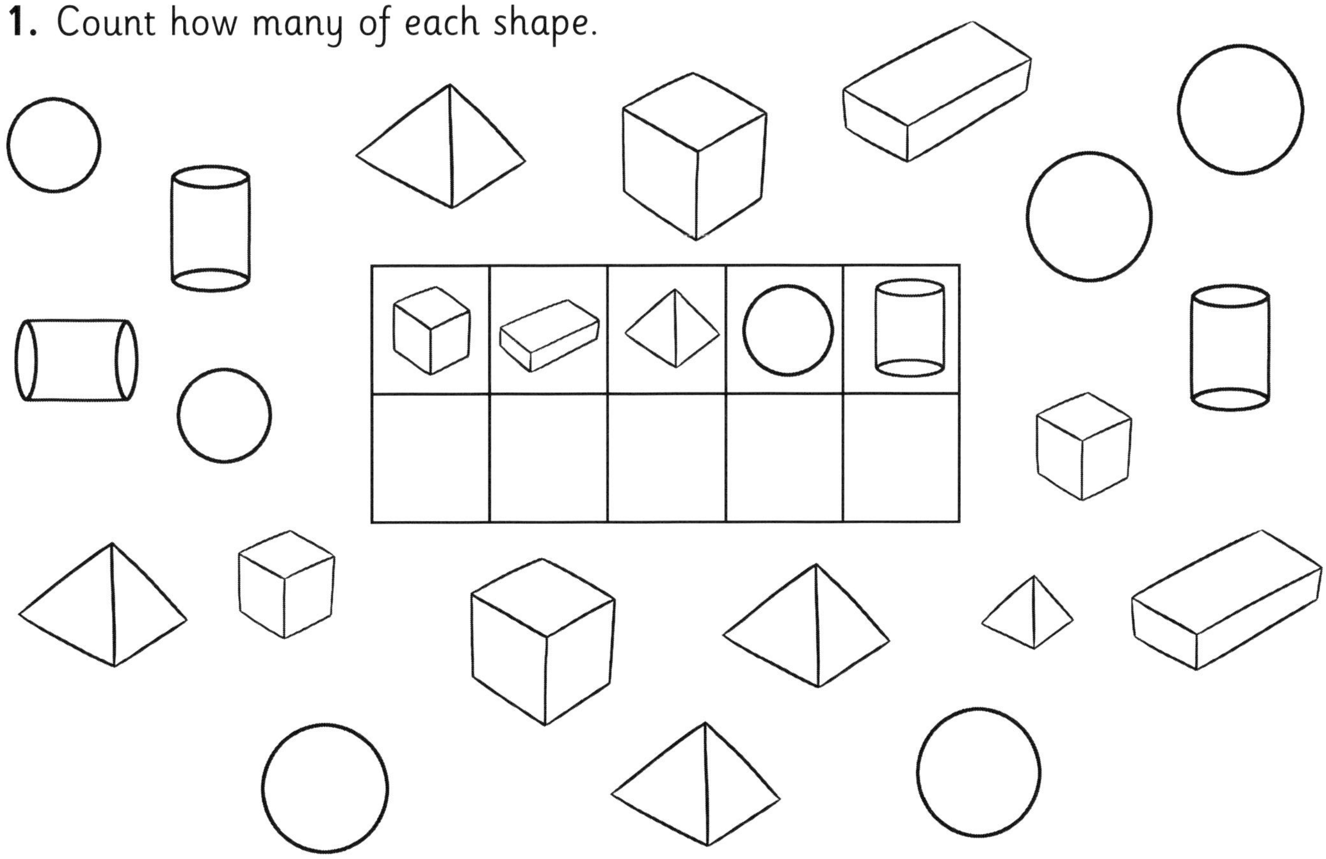

2. Count the matching shapes on the table top.

Count how many of each shape.

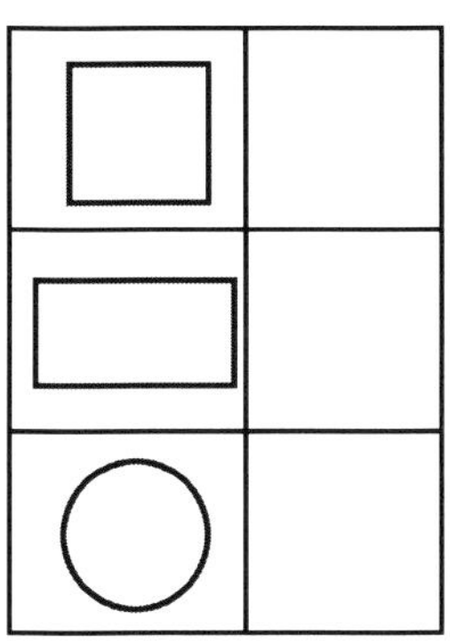

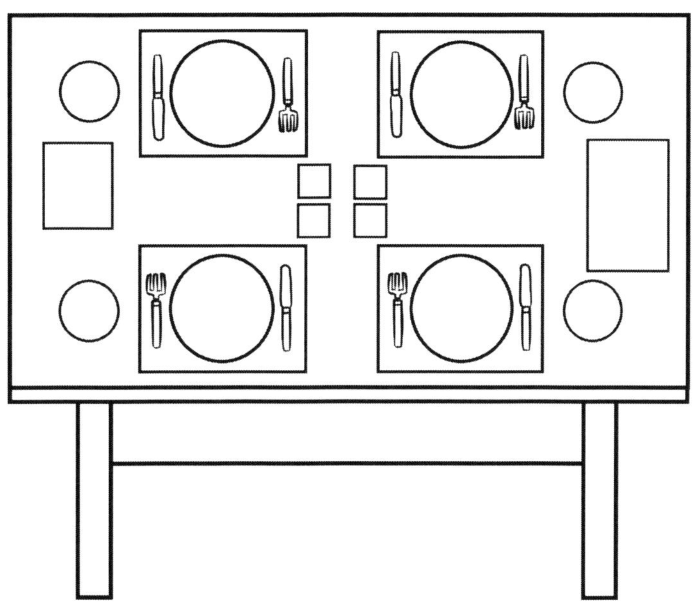

Counting shapes

Go on a circle hunt around the house and see how many your child can find. Give them a piece of paper and pencil so they can draw a small circle each time they see one. When the hunt has finished, they can then count their circles to work out the total.

1.7 Let's count (4)

Count groups of up to 10 objects

1. Draw spots on each dragon to match the numbers.

2. A farmer wants five chickens in each pen.
Draw around groups of five chickens.

3. Colour the purses with 10 coins.

Coin sort

Empty your purse of all the coins (and find other coins around the house!) and ask your child to sort them so there are 10 of each coin. Count the coins and talk about the similarities and differences your child can see.

You will need:
coins of different denominations (at least 10 of each).

1.8 Let's count (5)

Count and recognise numbers to 10, including zero

1. Draw some leaves on each tree. Make each tree different.
Write the number of leaves in each box.

2. How many flowers are in each vase?

3. Draw the apples in the baskets to match each label.

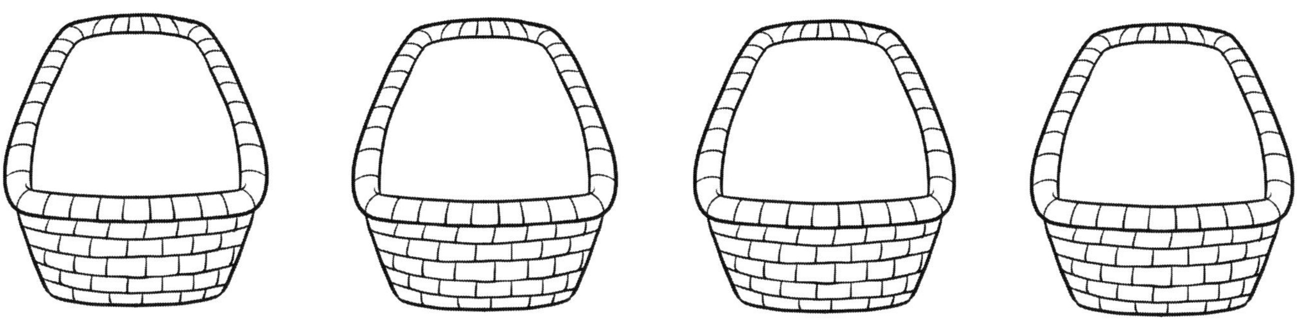

6 0 10 9

Counting fruit

Make a collection of between five and 10 biscuits or pieces of fruit (two different kinds) on one plate. Talk about how many of each kind there are and how many there are altogether. Move them, one at a time, under a cloth until they are all out of sight, counting back as you do. Emphasise the word 'zero' to show there are no pieces of fruit or biscuits left on the plate. Repeat two or three times.

You will need:
fruit or biscuits, a plate, a cloth.

1.9 Let's count (6)

Count and partition numbers to 10

1. Count these. Write how many of each.

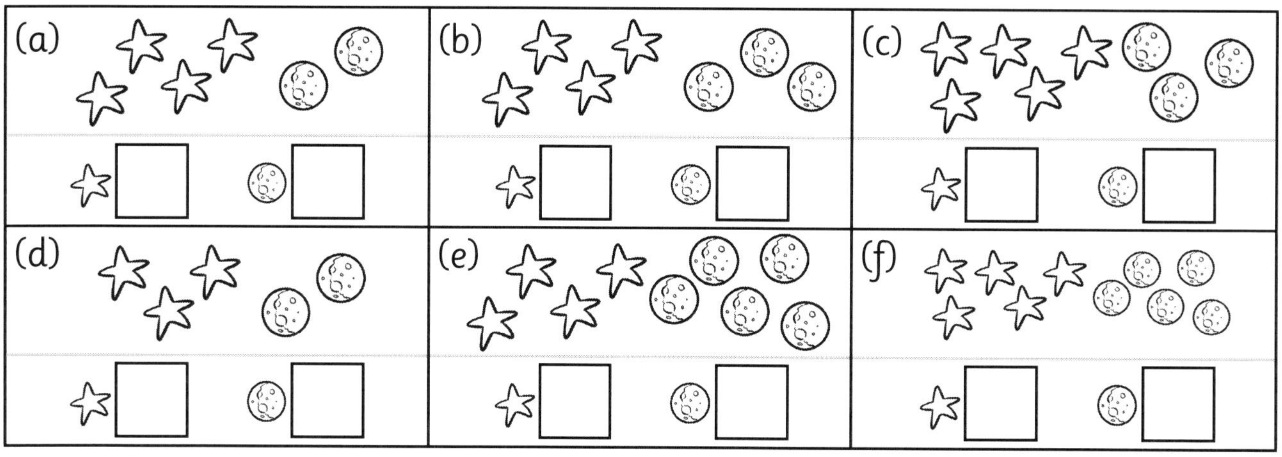

2. How many spots are on each domino?

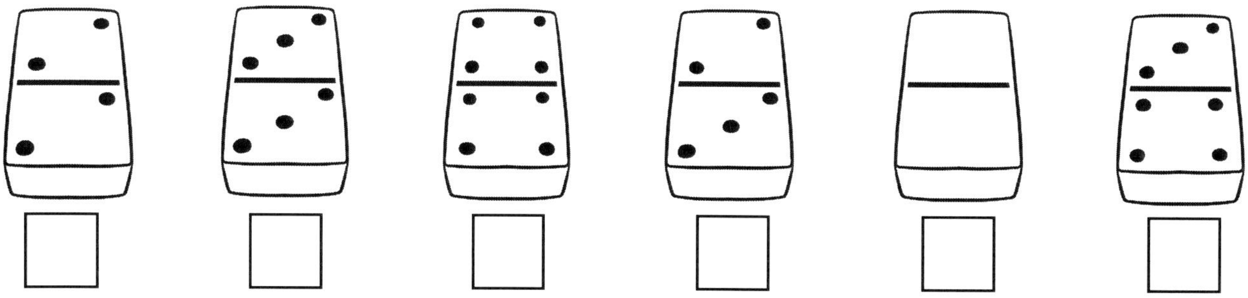

3. Draw dots on the other side of each of these to make the number.

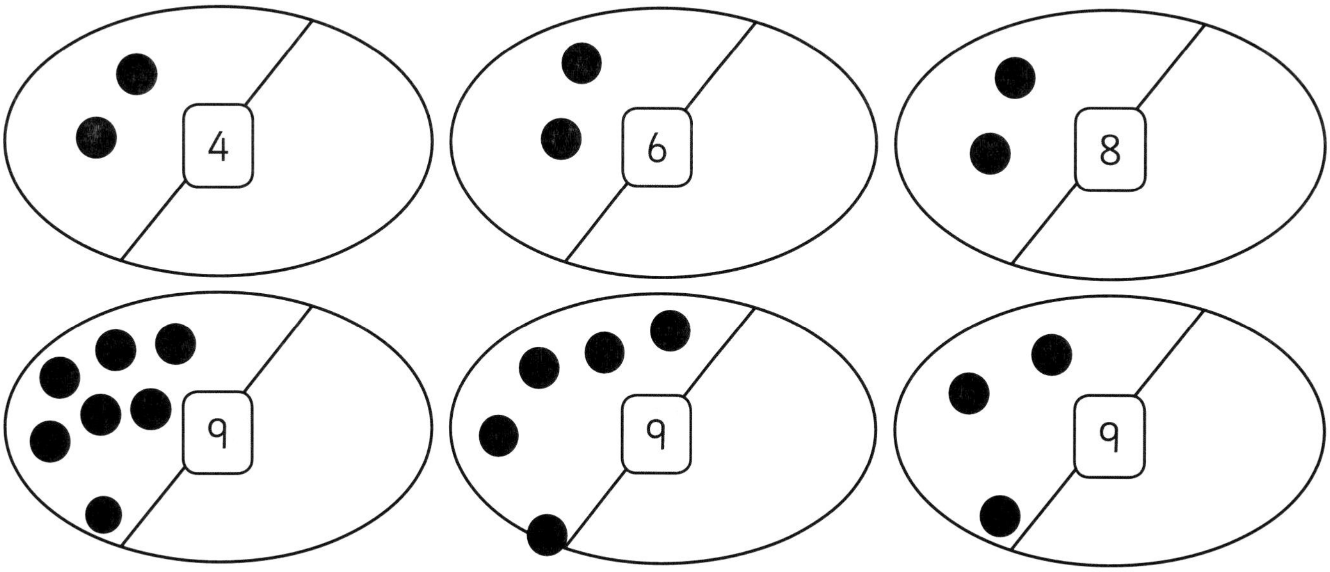

Flip the cups

Place five (if possible identical) cups or beakers in a row. Turn one over at a time and show that 4 and 1, 3 and 2, 2 and 3, 1 and 4 all make 5. Repeat with different numbers of cups.

You will need:
five identical cups or beakers.

1.10 Counting and ordering numbers (1)

Count and order numbers to 10

1. Look at the picture and fill in the boxes.

There are □ animals.

The  is □ in the line.

The  is □ in the line.

The  is □ in the line.

The  is □ in the line.

The  is □ in the line.

The  is □ in the line.

2. Count and colour. Start from the left.

Colour two □ ⟶ □ □ □ □ □

Colour the second □ ⟶ □ □ □ □ □

Colour three △ ⟶ △ △ △ △ △

Colour the third △ ⟶ △ △ △ △ △

Colour four ○ ⟶ ○ ○ ○ ○ ○

Colour the fourth ○ ⟶ ○ ○ ○ ○ ○

Colour five □ ⟶ □ □ □ □ □

Colour the fifth □ ⟶ □ □ □ □ □

In a line

Ask your child to put some of their toy animals or cars into a line with one behind the other. Ask which is first, which is second, which is last and so on. Make sure all the toys face the same direction and explain that if your child turns the toys around, the order is changed, with first becoming last. What is the position of each toy now?

You will need:
toy animals or cars.

1.11 Counting and ordering numbers (2)

Write ordinal numbers to 10

1. Join these to show the order of length starting from the longest. One has been done for you.

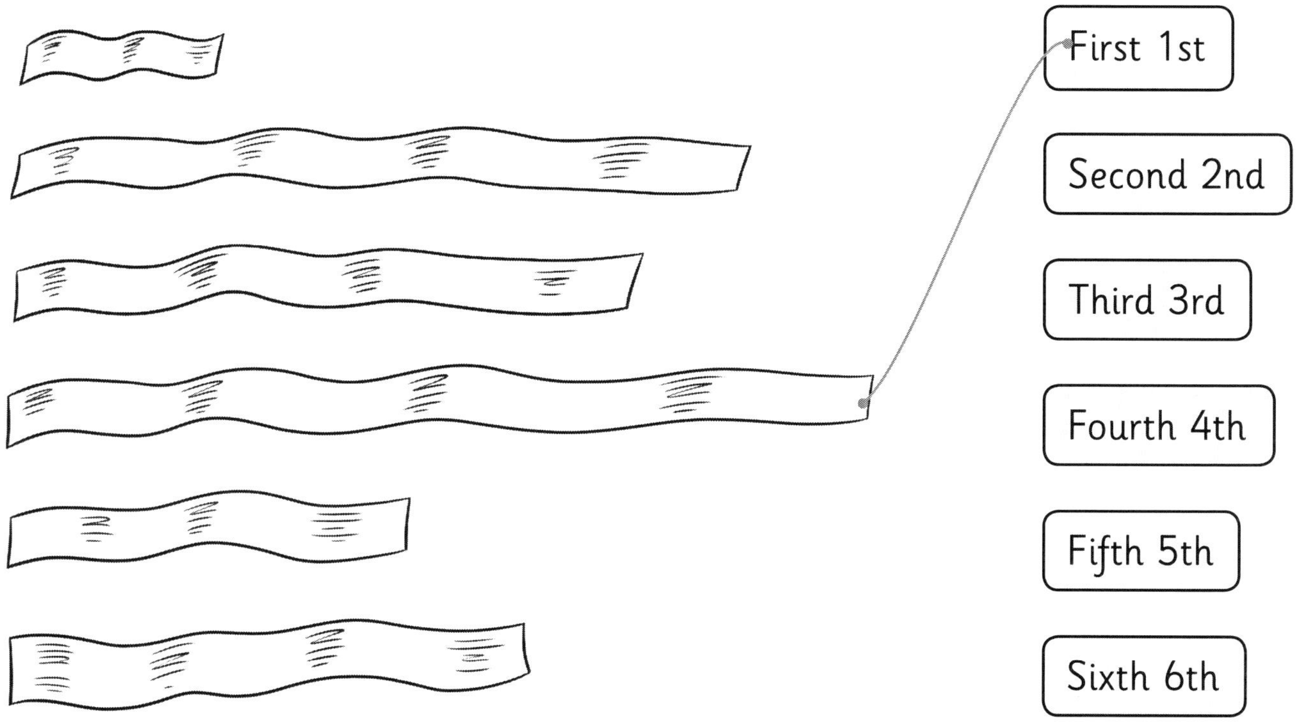

2. Put these pictures in the correct order. Choose from: 1st, 2nd, 3rd and 4th.

Dressing in order

When dressing in the morning ask your child to use the words 'first, second, third, fourth ...' and so on to show the order they put their clothes on. You can also ask what they put on first, or what they put on last once they are dressed.

1.12 Let's compare (1)

Compare sets to find more or fewer

1. Count these. Put a tick (✓) next to the set that has **more**.

(a)  ☐

 ☐

(b)  ☐

 ☐

2. Colour the set that has the **most**.

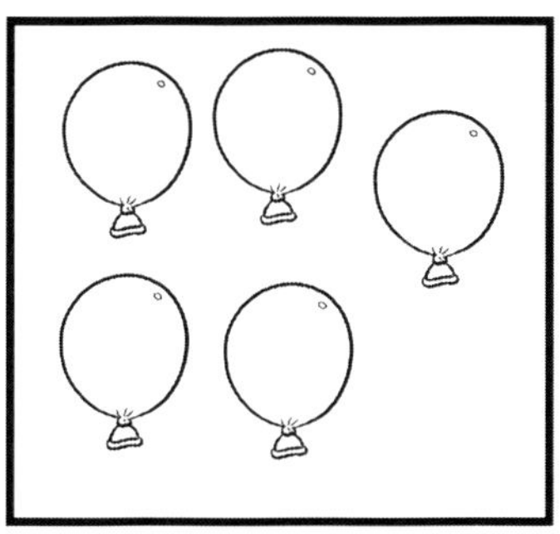

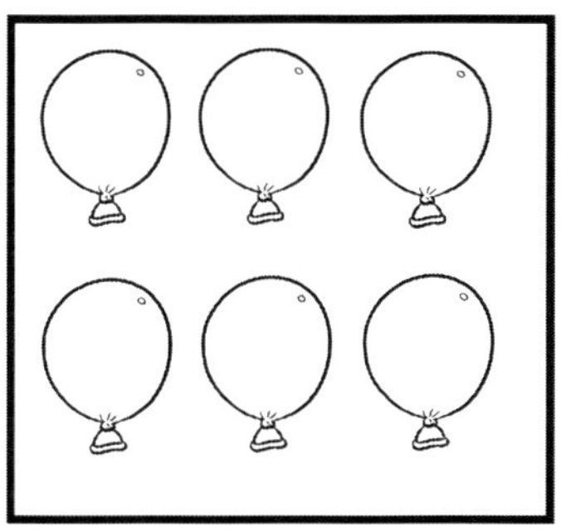

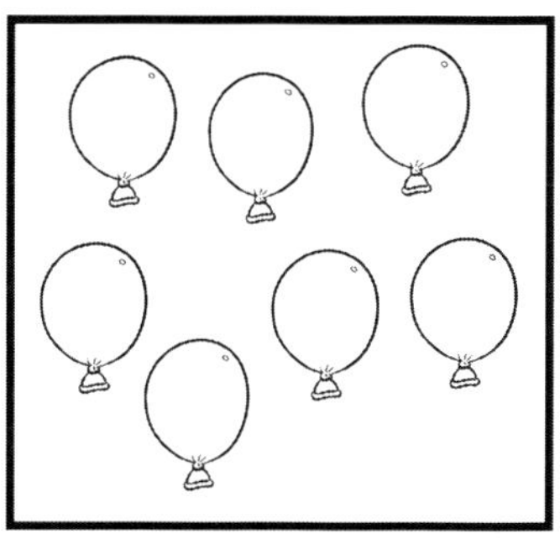

3. Draw some balls in the bag so there are **fewer** than in the box.

I have drawn ☐ balls.

There are ☐ fewer balls in the bag than in the box.

Which has more?

Play a game of 'Which has more?' Put some beads or pegs into two bags so that your child does not know how many are in each bag. Ask them to look in the bags and guess which one has more. Once they have guessed they take out the objects and line them up to compare. If they are correct they take one of the objects and if not, you have an object. Keep playing to see who collects five objects first.

You will need:
beads or pegs,
2 bags.

1.13 Let's compare (2)

Compare sets using greater than or less than

1. Write <, > or = in the ◯ for each of these.

> is greater than	< is less than	= is equal to

5 ◯ 4

3 ◯ 5

6 ◯ 6

6 ◯ 5

2. Count and complete these.

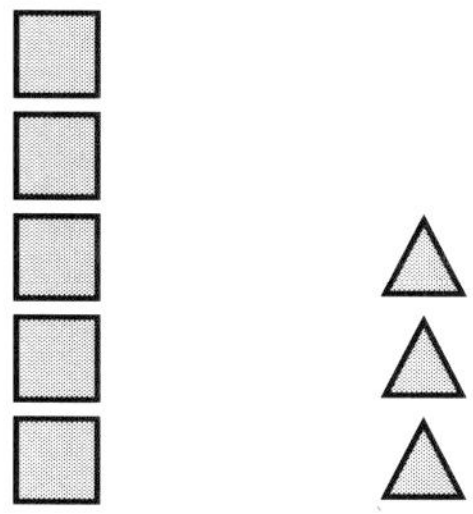

☐ ◯ ☐

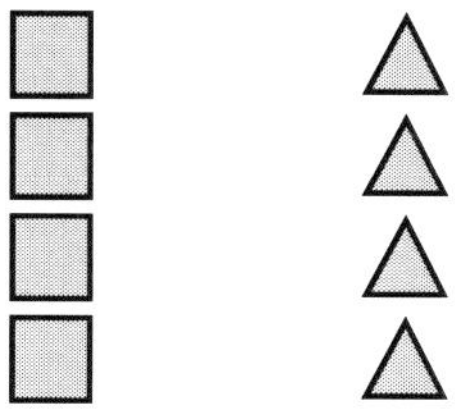

☐ ◯ ☐

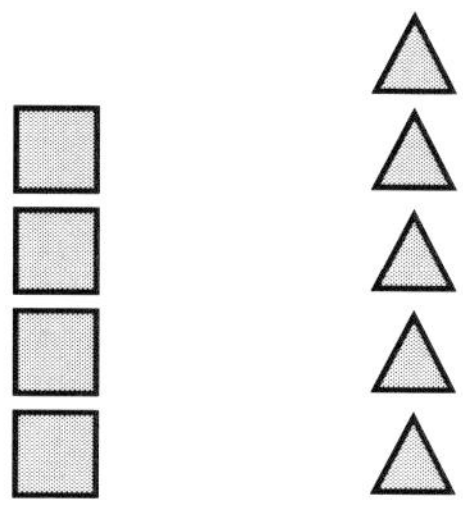

☐ ◯ ☐

3. Choose your own numbers to complete these.

6 > ☐ 10 > ☐ ☐ > 8 ☐ > 2

4 < ☐ 7 < ☐ ☐ < 5 ☐ < 9

Greater than and less than

Draw a large > on a piece of paper. Put two piles of small objects on a table with a space between them. Ask your child to count the objects and decide which way around to put the > symbol so that it is correct. Repeat, changing the number of objects in the piles and the direction of the symbol.

1.14 The number line

Identify numbers to 10 on a number line

Information for parents:

This is how your child is being taught to write numbers.

1. Trace over the numbers on this number line.

0 1 2 3 4 5 6 7 8 9 10

2. Write the missing numbers on these number lines.

(a) 1 ☐ 3 ☐ ☐ 6

(b) 4 5 6 ☐ ☐ ☐ 10

(c) 0 ☐ 2 3 ☐ ☐ 6 7

(d) ☐ ☐ 5 6 ☐ 8 9

3. Circle these numbers on the number line.

6 3 10 5 9

0 1 2 3 4 5 6 7 8 9 10

Write the numbers in order, starting with the least.

☐ ☐ ☐ ☐ ☐

Number line

Draw a 0–10 number line on a piece of paper and use three objects to cover three numbers without your child seeing them. They then try to work out the missing numbers. Take turns so you have to work out the missing numbers, explaining how you know.

2.1 Number bonds

Represent number bonds to 10

1. Circle the objects and complete the number bonds.

7: 2, □

7: 3, □

7: 4, □

7: 5, □

2. Complete the number bond and shade the circles to match.

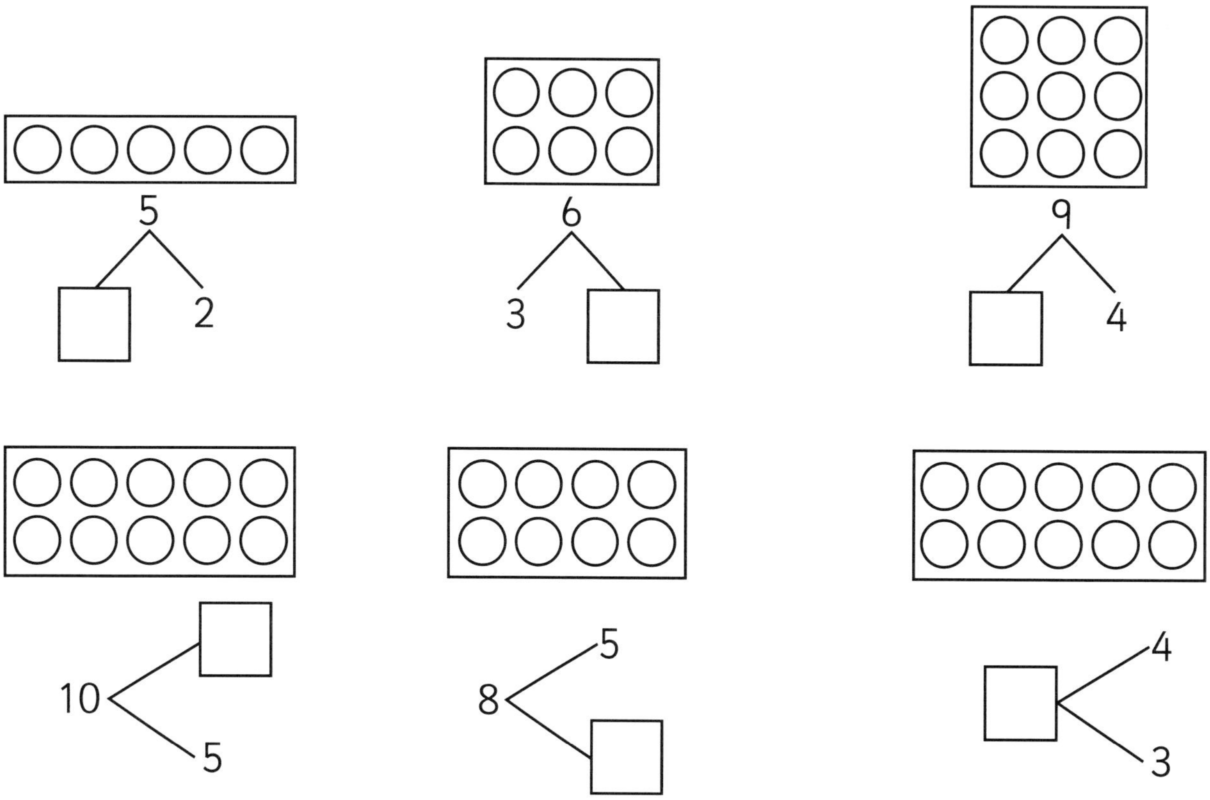

Take 5

Give your child six small countable objects. Ask them to put the objects into two groups, so, for example four and two. Say: *Four and two make six* and then ask if they can split the objects in any other way. Find all the possible ways of making six and then repeat for seven.

2.2 Addition (1)

Add pairs of numbers with a total to 10

1. Add these. Fill in the boxes.

(a)

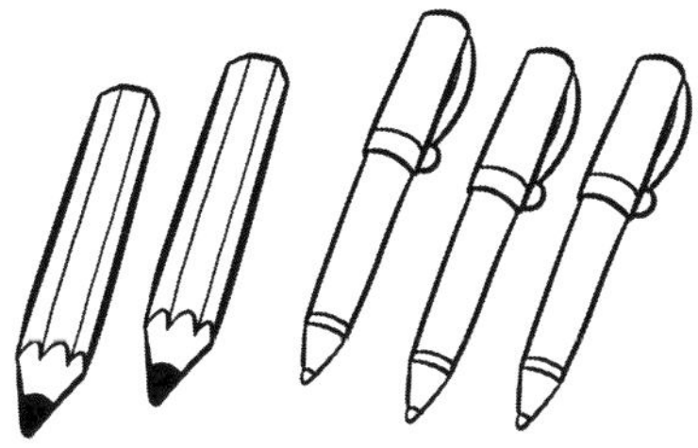

2 + 3 = ☐

3 + 2 = ☐

(b)

4 + ☐ = ☐

☐ + 4 = ☐

(c)

☐ + ☐ = ☐

☐ + ☐ = ☐

(d)

☐ + ☐ = ☐

☐ + ☐ = ☐

2. Join these to the correct total.

1 + 5

3 + 3

= 5

3 + 2

4 + 2

1 + 4

= 6

2 + 3

2 + 4

4 + 1

Making 7

Write an + sign on a piece of paper and place it on a table. Ask your child to take seven small objects and put them in two groups either side of the sign. They say the sum, for example three add four is seven. Repeat this, showing all the pairs that are equal to seven. Repeat for eight.

2.3 Addition (2)

Add pairs of numbers with a total to 10

1. Write each addition sentence.

(a) 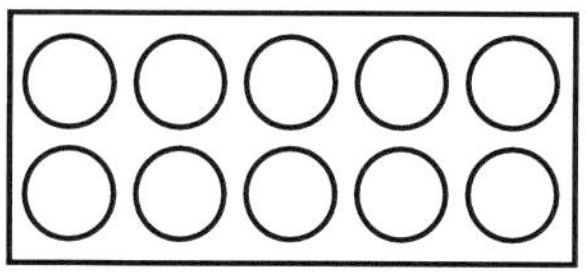

0 + [10] = 10

(b) 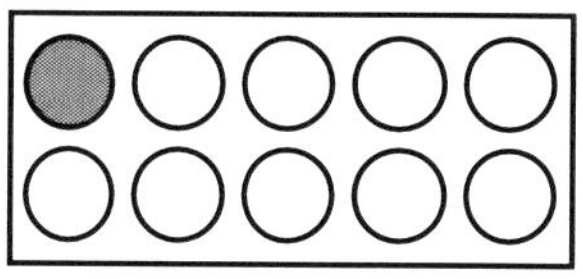

1 + [ ] = 10

(c) 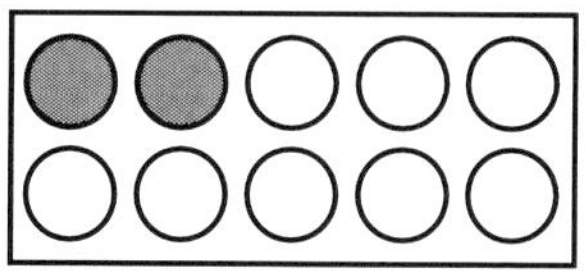

2 + [ ] = 10

(d) 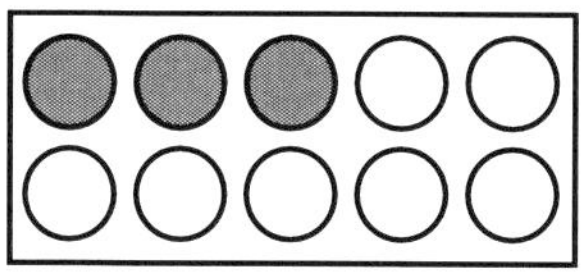

[ ] + [ ] = 10

(e) 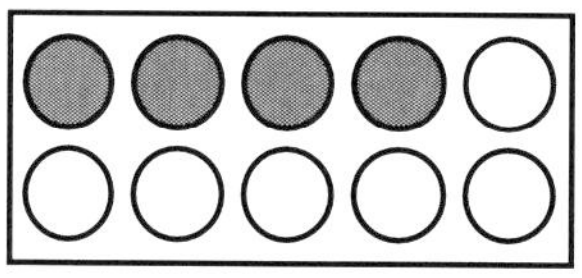

[ ] + [ ] = 10

(f) 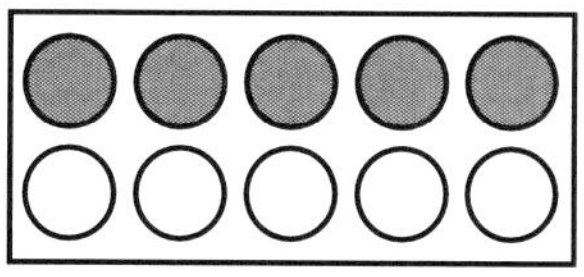

[ ] + [ ] = 10

2. Colour the dots to show different pairs of numbers that add to a sum of 8.

(a) 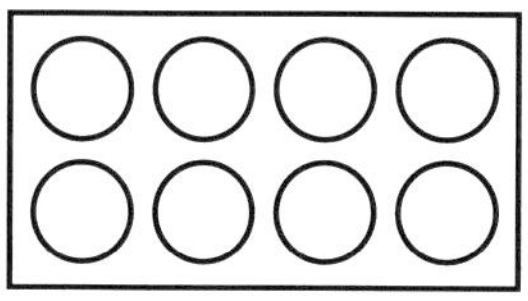

[ ] + [ ] = 8

(b) 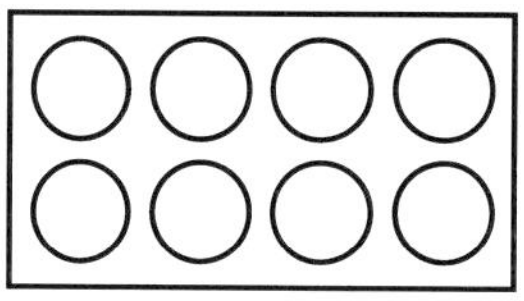

[ ] + [ ] = 8

(c) 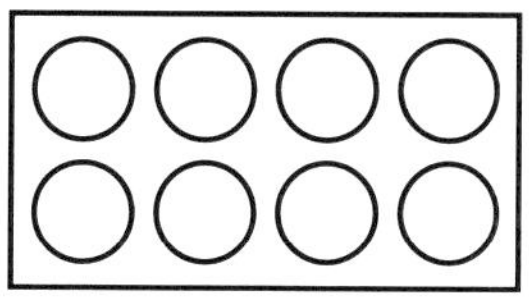

[ ] + [ ] = 8

(d) 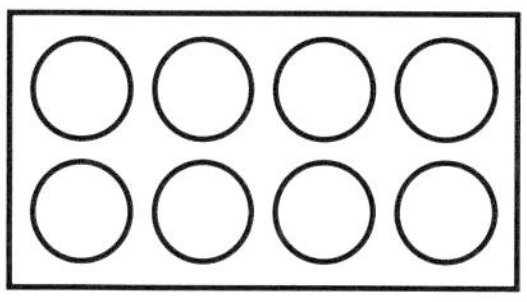

[ ] + [ ] = 8

(e) 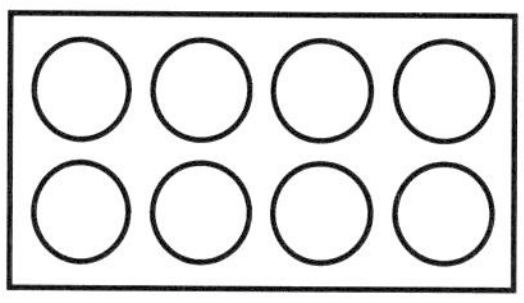

[ ] + [ ] = 8

(f) 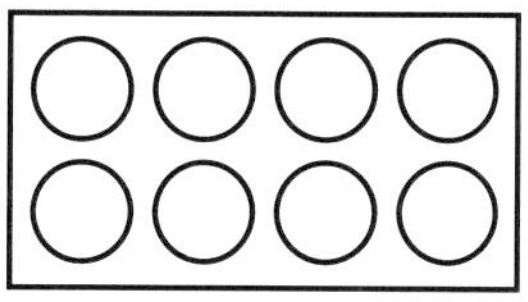

[ ] + [ ] = 8

3. Add these.

(a) 4 + 1 = [ ]　　(b) 3 + 6 = [ ]　　(c) 5 + 2 = [ ]

(d) 2 + 4 = [ ]　　(e) 3 + 3 = [ ]　　(f) 4 + 5 = [ ]

Pairs

Prepare a set of 12 cards with 0–5 written twice. Shuffle and place them face down on a table. Play a game of pairs with your child with the aim to turn over a pair of cards with a total of five. The winner is the player that collects the most pairs.

2.4 Addition (3)

Add to 10 by combining

1. Write the addition sentences for these.

(a)

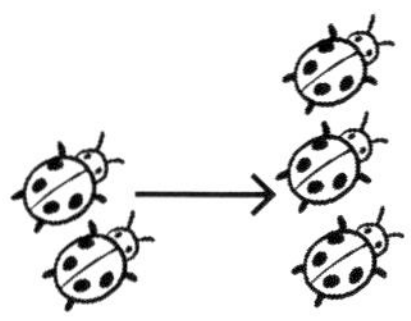

[2] + [3] = [ ]

(b)

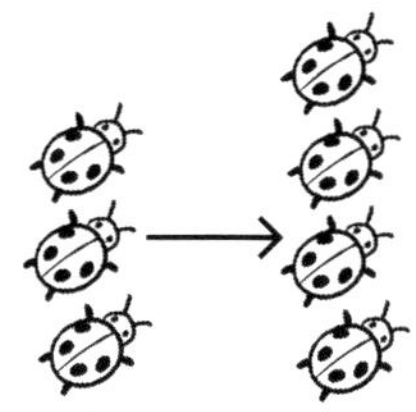

[ ] + [ ] = [ ]

(c)

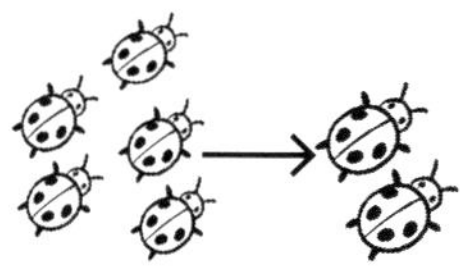

[ ] + [ ] = [ ]

(d)

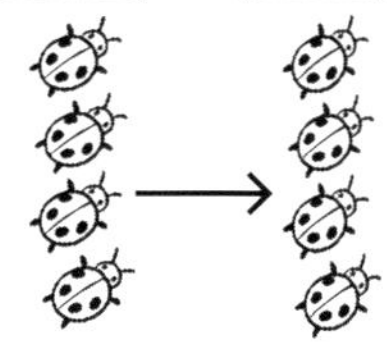

[ ] + [ ] = [ ]

2. Draw 2 more bugs on each leaf. How many are on each leaf now? Write the addition sentence under each leaf.

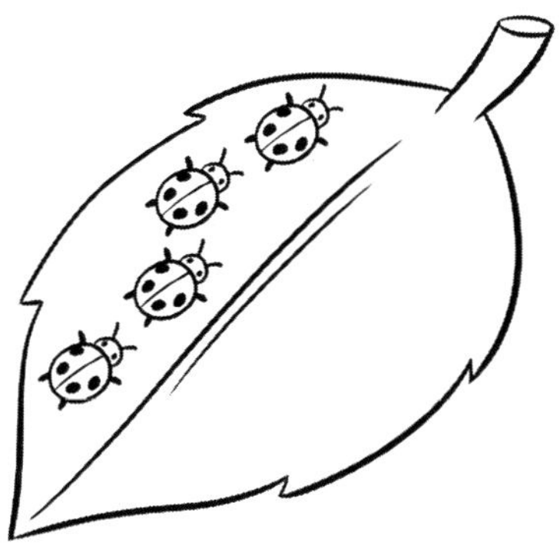

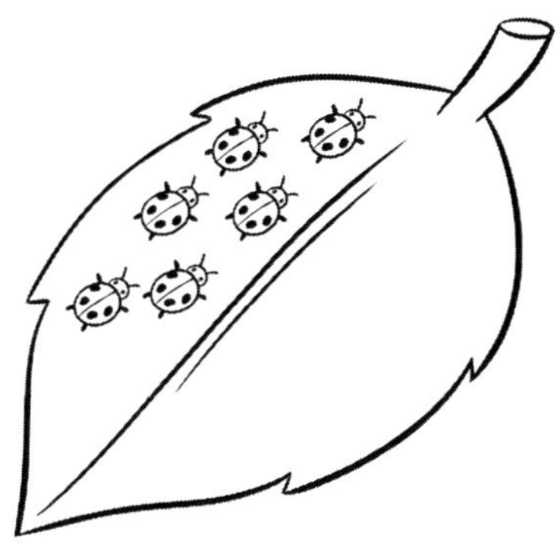

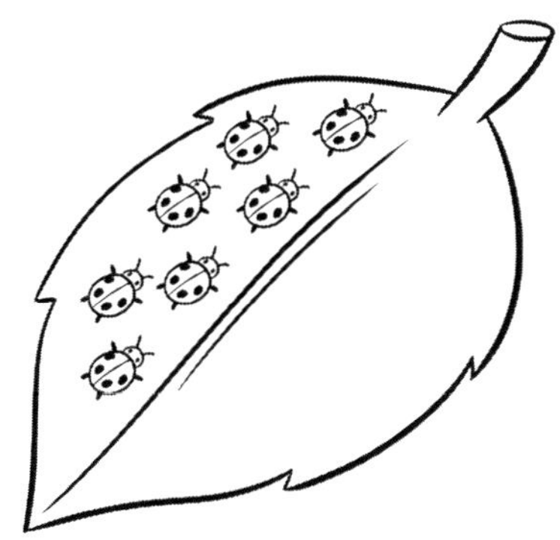

(a) [4] + [ ] = [ ] (b) [ ] + [ ] = [ ] (c) [ ] + [ ] = [ ]

3. Complete these.

(a) 3 —+ 2→ [ ] (b) 7 —+ 2→ [ ] (c) 4 —+ 2→ [ ]

(d) 5 —+ 1→ [ ] (e) 1 —+ 4→ [ ] (f) 6 —+ 3→ [ ]

Rows of tins

You will need: 10 food tins.

Use up to 10 tins from your kitchen cupboard to practice adding. Ask your child to make a row using up to five of the tins and say how many there are. They then make a new row with some of the other tins and add the two rows together. Repeat to make different totals.

2.5 Let's talk and calculate (I)

Write addition sentences with totals to 10

1. Draw the total number of flowers. Write the addition sentences.

(a)

$\boxed{2} + \boxed{3} = \boxed{}$

(b)

$\boxed{} + \boxed{} = \boxed{}$

(c)

$\boxed{} + \boxed{} = \boxed{}$

(d)

$\boxed{} + \boxed{} = \boxed{}$

2. Fill in the boxes.

(a) $3 \xrightarrow{+2} \boxed{}$

(b) $4 \xrightarrow{+5} \boxed{}$

(c) $6 \xrightarrow{+3} \boxed{}$

(d) $2 \xrightarrow{+\boxed{}} 3$

(e) $6 \xrightarrow{+\boxed{}} 8$

(f) $5 \xrightarrow{+\boxed{}} 10$

(g) $\boxed{} \xrightarrow{+2} 4$

(h) $\boxed{} \xrightarrow{+1} 9$

(i) $\boxed{} \xrightarrow{+3} 7$

Adding words

Encourage your child to use the language of addition in their daily play both in and out of the home. Listen out for your child using any of the following words: *add*, *total*, *altogether*, *sum*, *together*, *adding more*, *increase*. Ask them to show you what they mean using counters or cubes and allow them plenty of time to explain in their own words.

2.6 Subtraction (1)

Subtract within 10 by taking away

1. Look at the picture and write the sentences.

(a) 4 subtract 1 is ☐

4 – 1 = ☐

(b) 8 subtract 3 is ☐

8 – 3 = ☐

(c) 6 subtract 2 is ☐

6 – 2 = ☐

(d) 8 subtract 2 is ☐

8 – 2 = ☐

2. Cross these out to match the subtraction. Write the answer. One has been done for you.

(a) ○○○○✗

5 – 1 = ☐

(b) ○○○○○

5 – 2 = ☐

(c) ○○○○○

5 – 3 = ☐

(d) ○○○○○○

6 – 4 = ☐

(e) ○○○○○○

6 – 3 = ☐

(f) ○○○○○○

6 – 2 = ☐

Take from 10

Put out 10 small items for your child to subtract from. Ask them to roll a dice (a dotted one is good) and remove that number of items from the group of 10. They repeat this with the aim to try and subtract and leave zero. Try to avoid always saying 'take away', use the word 'subtract' instead so you are using accurate mathematical language.

You will need: a dice.

2.7 Subtraction (2)

Subtract within 10 using known addition bonds

1. Look at the pictures and write the sentences.

(a) There are 6 bugs altogether

4 ☐ How many?

6 – 4 = ☐

(b) There are 8 bugs altogether

3 ☐ How many?

8 – ☐ = ☐

(c) There are 9 bugs altogether

5 ☐ How many?

☐ – ☐ = ☐

(d) There are 7 bugs altogether

2 ☐ How many?

☐ – ☐ = ☐

2. Fill in the boxes.

(a) 3 —(– 1)→ ☐

(b) 5 —(– 4)→ ☐

(c) 4 —(– 2)→ ☐

(d) 6 —(– 4)→ ☐

(e) 4 —(– 3)→ ☐

(f) 7 —(– 5)→ ☐

(g) 5 —(– ☐)→ 3

(h) 9 —(– ☐)→ 6

(i) 8 —(– ☐)→ 2

Hidden numbers

You need a cup and some small items such as paper clips or coins. Put 10 out on a table and ask your child to count them. Then cover three of them with the cup without your child seeing. They count the number of items left on the table to work out the number of items hidden under the cup. Repeat for different numbers.

You will need:
a cup, 10 small objects.

2.8 Subtraction (3)

Subtract within 10 using known addition bonds

1. Cross these out to match the subtraction. Write the answer.

(a) 

4 – 1 = 3

(b) 

6 – □ = 2

(c) 

8 – 3 = □

(d) 

5 – 2 = □

(e) 

7 – 3 = □

(f) 

9 – □ = 6

2. Write the subtraction sentence for these.

(a) 

□ ○ □ = □

(b) 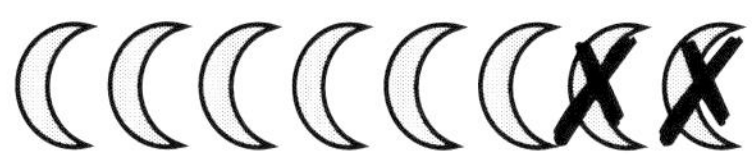

□ ○ □ = □

(c) 

□ ○ □ = □

(d) 

□ ○ □ = □

Leave 2

Explore the different subtraction facts that have an answer of 2. Use small objects to 10 and ask how many need to be subtracted to leave 2. Write the facts in order and ask your child what they notice: 10 – 8, 9 – 7, 8 – 6, 7 – 5 and so on.

2.9 Let's talk and calculate (II)

Interpret word problems using subtraction facts to 10

1. Read these and complete the number sentences.

(a) There were 5 fish in a tank. 2 were taken out. How many fish are left in the tank?

□ ○ □ = □

(b) There were 6 balls in a shop. 2 were sold. How many balls are left in the shop?

□ ○ □ = □

(c) There are 8 flowers altogether. 3 of them are . How many  are there?

□ ○ □ = □

(d) There are 7 hats in total. There are 5 . How many  are there?

□ ○ □ = □

2. Complete these.

(a) 8 $\xrightarrow{-4}$ □

(b) 10 $\xrightarrow{-5}$ □

(c) 6 $\xrightarrow{-3}$ □

(d) 5 $\xrightarrow{-\square}$ 2

(e) 7 $\xrightarrow{-\square}$ 2

(f) 9 $\xrightarrow{-\square}$ 2

(g) □ $\xrightarrow{-3}$ 1

(h) □ $\xrightarrow{-3}$ 2

(i) □ $\xrightarrow{-3}$ 3

3. Calculate.

(a) 3 – 3 = □

(b) 5 – 4 = □

(c) 7 – 4 = □

(d) 8 – 5 = □

(e) 9 – 6 = □

(f) 10 – 3 = □

Subtraction words

Encourage your child to use the language of subtraction in their daily play and when in and out of the home. Listen out for your child using any of the following words: *subtract, subtracting, take away, fewer, less, minus, reduce, difference*. Ask them to show you what they mean using counters, cubes or drawings.

2.10 Addition and subtraction

Use the inverse relationship between addition and subtraction with numbers to 10

1. Look at the pictures and write the number sentences.

(a)

6 + ☐ = ☐

(b)

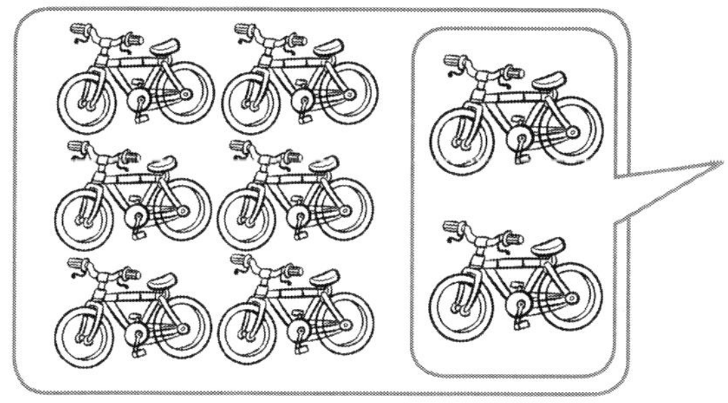

8 – ☐ = ☐

(c)

☐ + ☐ = ☐

(d)

☐ – ☐ = ☐

2. Fill in the boxes.

(a)

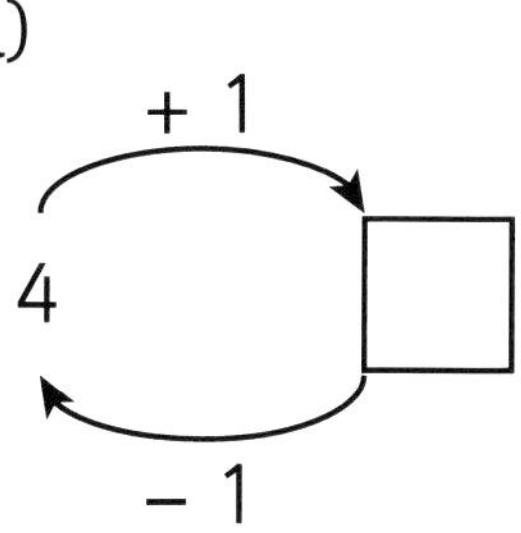

(b)

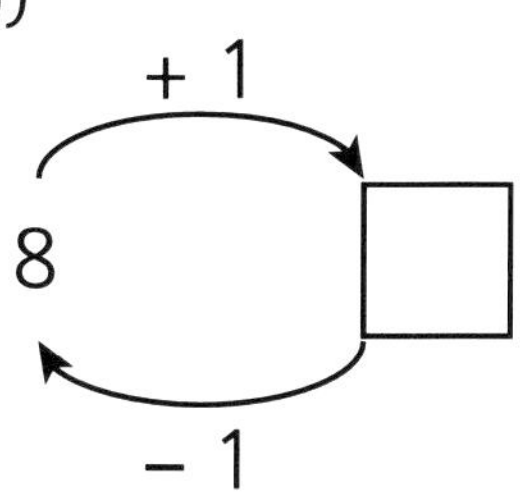

(c)

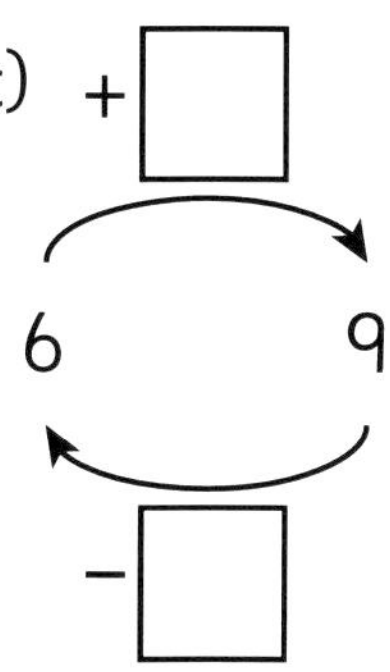

(d)

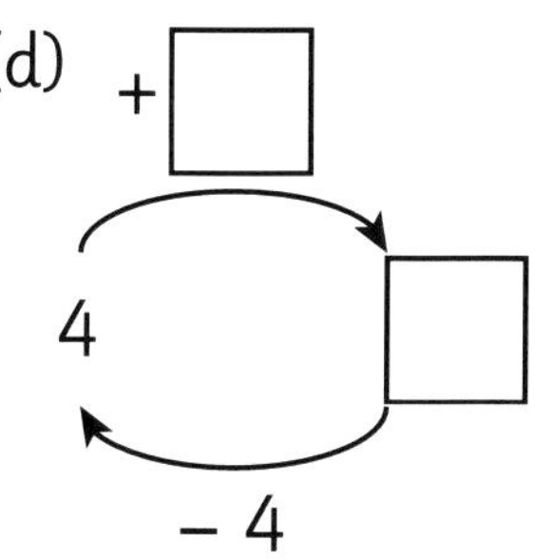

Back to the start

Reinforce the idea that addition and subtraction are inverse or opposite operations. Place up to seven objects on a table and count them. Then add three more. Ask how many would need to be taken away to get back to the first number. Repeat for different starting numbers.

2.11 Addition and subtraction using a number line

Add and subtract numbers to 10 using a number line

1. Calculate these.

(a)

+ ☐

2 + ☐ = 6

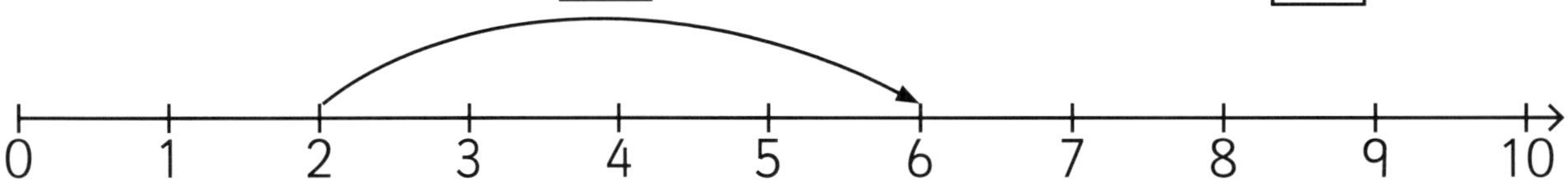

(b)

– ☐

8 – ☐ = ☐

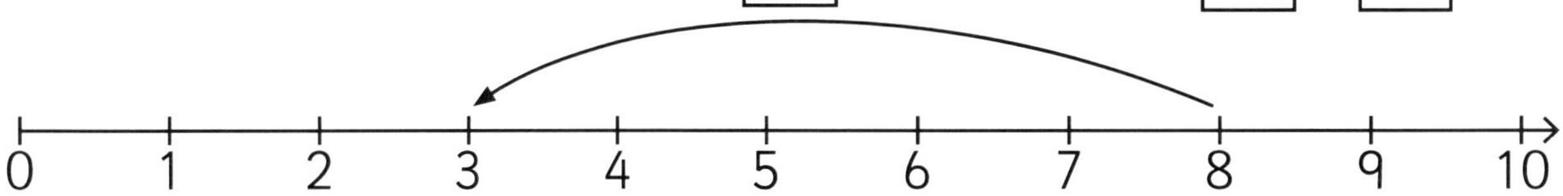

2. Draw the jumps on the number lines. Write the answers.

(a)

6 + 4 = ☐

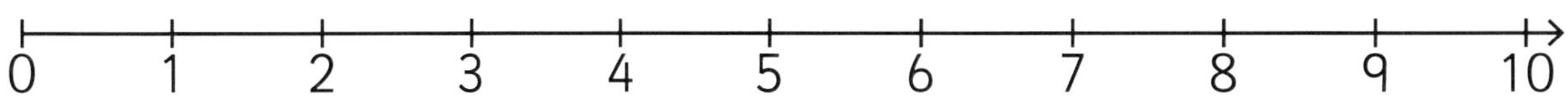

(b)

9 – 6 = ☐

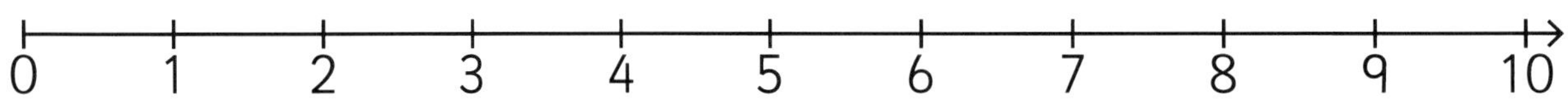

End of the line

Prepare a set of 12 cards with +1, +2, +3 and –1, –2, –3 each repeated twice. Draw a number line and play a game with your child. Each of you place a counter on 5, shuffle the cards and take turns to turn over the top card. Move your counter to match the instruction on the card. Your child is aiming to reach 10 before you reach 0.

2.12 Games of number 10

Solve problems for pairs of numbers that total 10

1. There are 10 ants in each picture. Write how many are hidden.

(a)

(b)

(c)

(d)

2. Join the pairs that total 10.

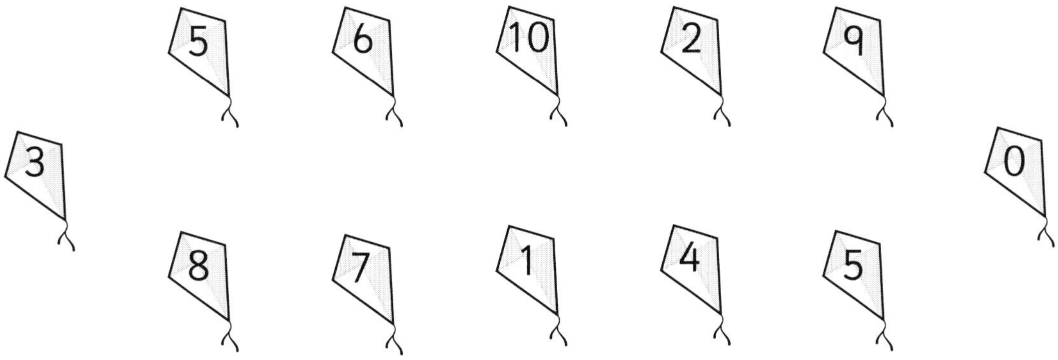

3. Write the missing numbers. They each total 10.

(a) $5 + \square$

(b) $\square + 6$

(c) $\square + 3$

(d) $1 + \square$

10

(e) $8 + \square$

Ten tennis

Play a game of ten tennis with your child. You 'serve' to start by saying any number to 10. You can show the number with your fingers to help. Your child then gives the number that makes a total of 10 as quickly as they can. If they are correct you give another number and continue playing. As soon as there is a mistake, swap and you child 'serves' a number.

2.13 Adding three numbers

Add three numbers with totals to 10

1. Look at the pictures and write the number sentences.

(a)

☐ + ☐ + ☐ = ☐

(b)

☐ + ☐ + ☐ = ☐

2. Look at the number line. Complete the number sentence.

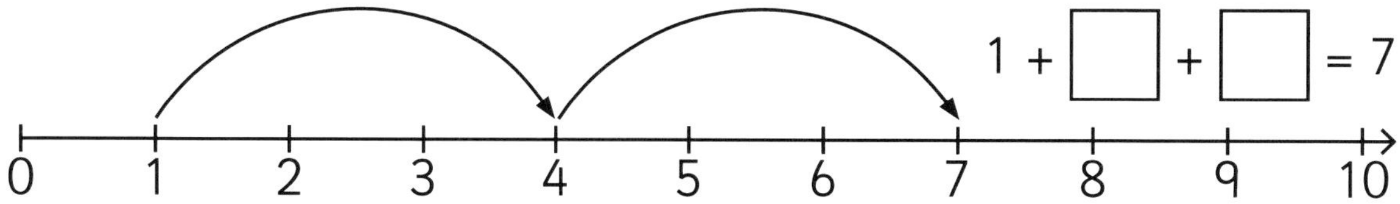

1 + ☐ + ☐ = 7

3. Use the number line to help you work out the total.

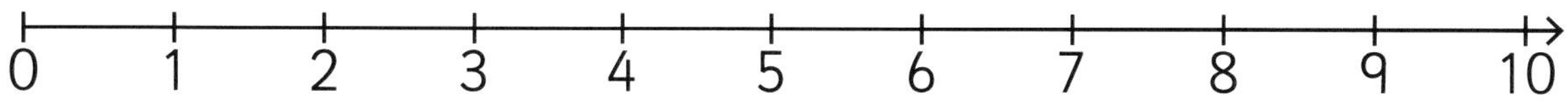

(a) 1 + 4 + 2 = ☐ (b) 3 + 5 + 1 = ☐ (c) 2 + 6 + 2 = ☐

(d) 5 + 0 + 4 = ☐ (e) 7 + 1 + 1 = ☐ (f) 3 + 3 + 2 = ☐

Reaching 10

Draw a 0–10 number line. Challenge your child to a race to reach 10 in exactly three jumps. Take turns to roll a dice. Move a counter or coin for each throw.

You will need: a dice.

2.14 Subtracting three numbers

Subtract smaller numbers from a number to 10

1. Use the pictures to help answer these.

(a)

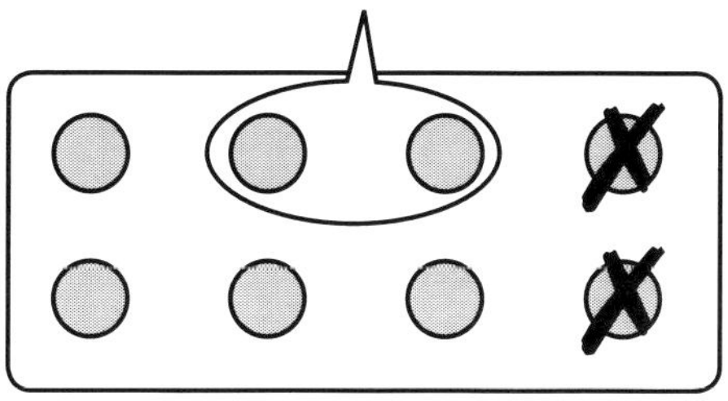

8 – 2 – 2 = ☐

(b)

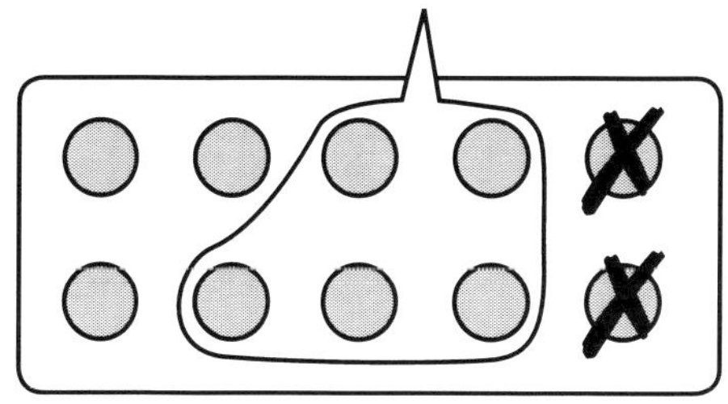

10 – ☐ – ☐ = ☐

2. Look at the number line. Complete the number sentence.

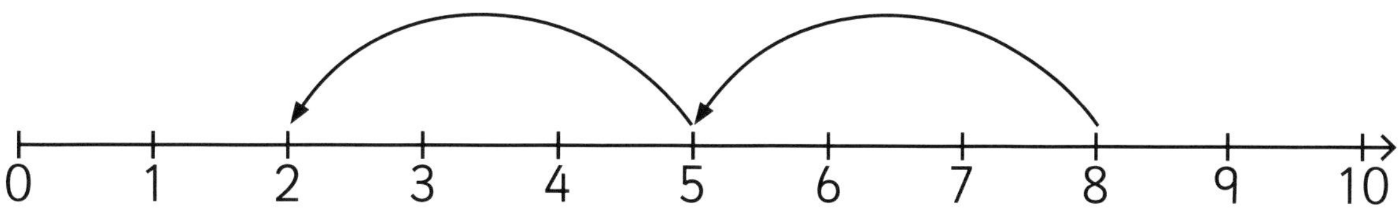

8 – ☐ – ☐ = 2

3. Use the number line to help you answer these.

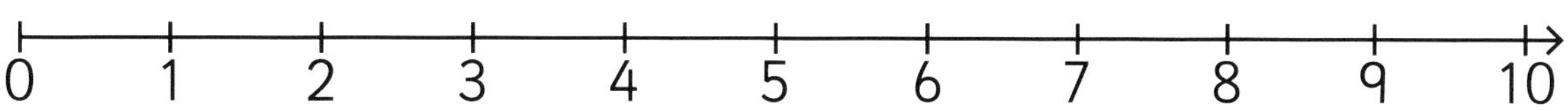

(a) 8 – 4 – 2 = ☐

(b) 10 – 3 – 4 = ☐

(c) 9 – 6 – 0 = ☐

(d) ☐ = 7 – 5 – 1

(e) ☐ = 8 – 1 – 6

(f) ☐ = 6 – 4 – 2

Reaching zero

Draw a 0–10 number line and place a counter or coin at 10. Ask your child to reach zero in two jumps. For example, they could jump back 7 and then 3. Set rules such as 'I want a small jump then a big jump' or 'I want two jumps that are the same.'

2.15 Mixed addition and subtraction

Add and subtract three numbers within 10

1. Look at the number lines and complete these.

(a)

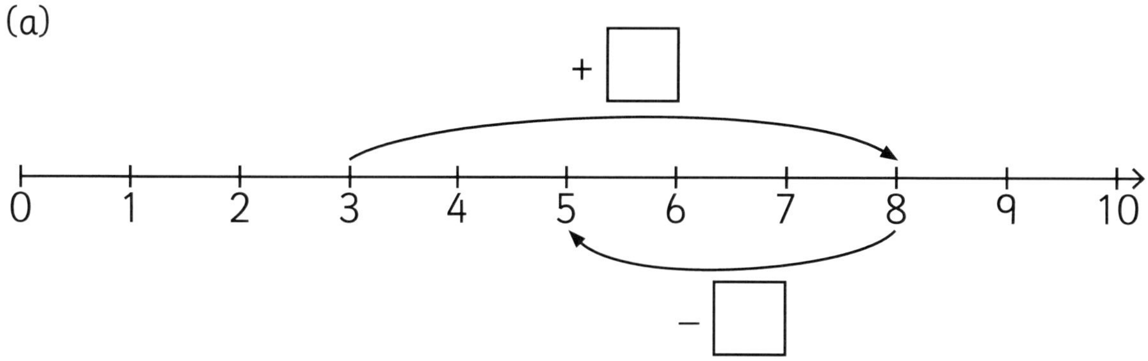

$3 + \square - \square = 5$

(b)

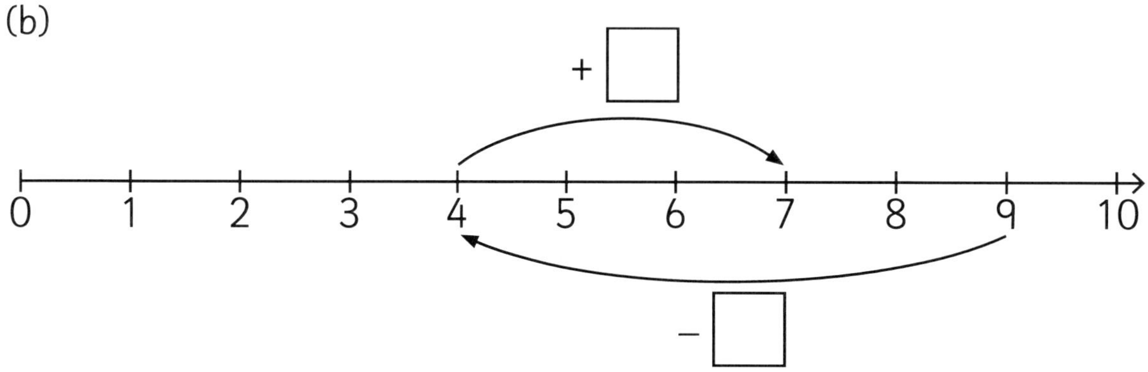

$9 - \square + \square = 7$

2. Fill in the ◯ with >, < or =.

(a) 8 – 4 + 2 ◯ 4

(b) 9 + 1 – 6 ◯ 4

(c) 7 – 6 + 3 ◯ 4

(d) 5 + 3 – 7 ◯ 4

1p shopping

Set up a 'Penny shop' with all items under 6p. The 'shopper' can only pay with 2p coins. The 'shopkeeper' can only use 1p coins as change. Price up different items and play at shopping so that totals are made and change given.

You will need:
1p and 2p coins, objects to 'sell'.

3.1 Numbers 11–20

Read and write numbers to 20

1. Write the missing numbers on this grid

1	2	3		5		7			10
11			14	15				19	

2. Count and write the numbers.

(a)

(b)

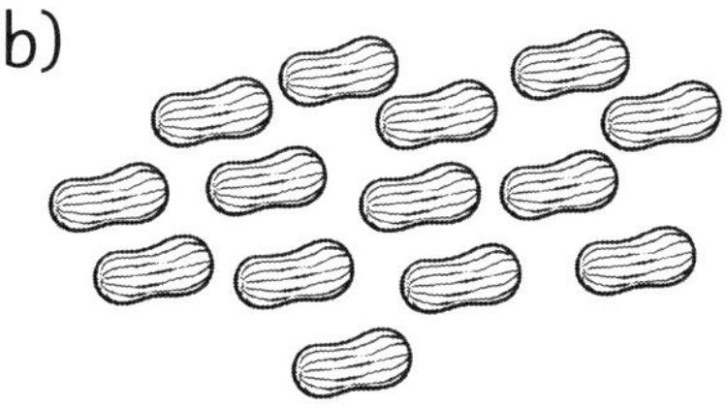

(c)

3. Write the missing numbers in these patterns.

(a)

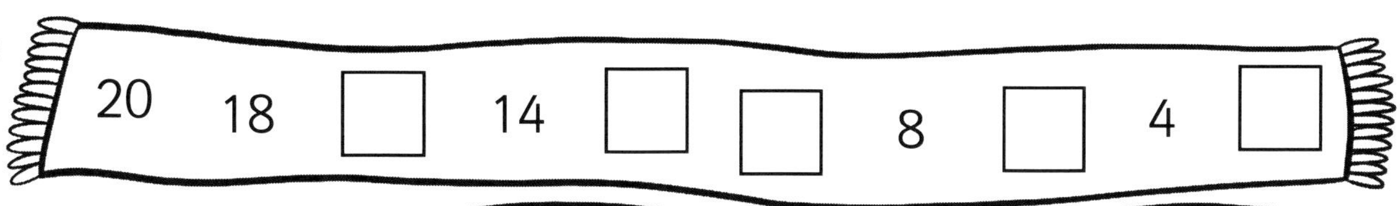

(b)

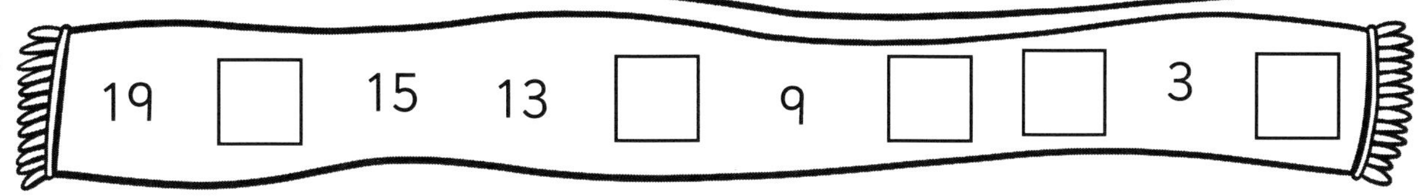

4. Colour the circles for each number.

(a)

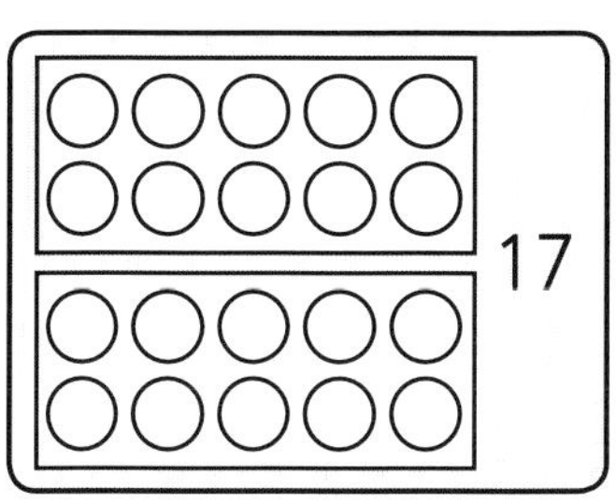

(b)

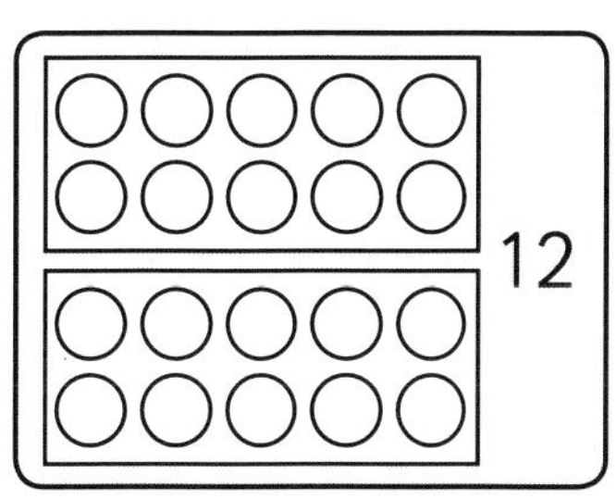

(c)

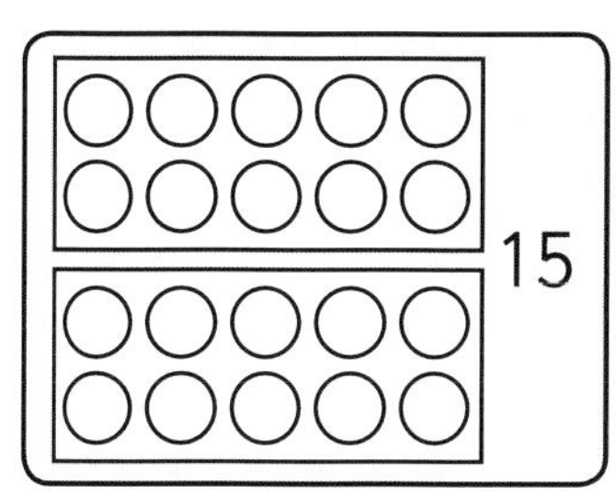

Number hunt

When you are out, ask your child to look for numbers between 10 and 20. Say them aloud and make sure they say them correctly. The numbers 11 and 12 can cause problems and from 13–19 emphasise the 'teen' for each number.

3.2 Tens and ones

Partition numbers into tens and ones

1. Count and join each set to the matching number.

(a)

16

19

15

18

(b)

(c)

(d)

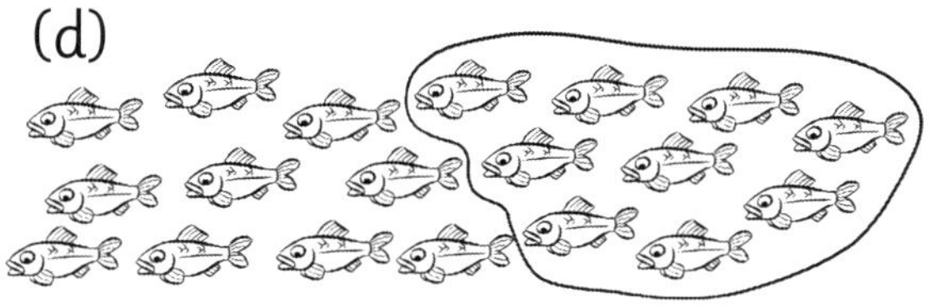

2. Split the numbers into tens and ones.

(a)

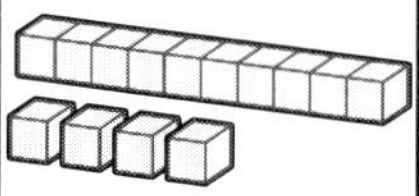

10 + 4 = ☐

(b)

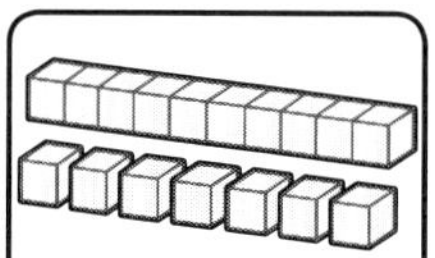

10 + 7 = ☐

(c)

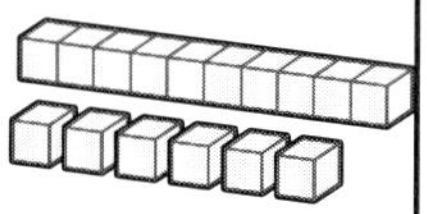

☐ + ☐ = ☐

(d)

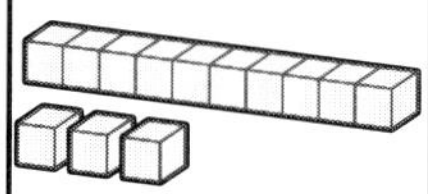

☐ + ☐ = ☐

3. Write the numbers in the boxes.

(a)

15 = 10 + ☐

19 = 10 + ☐

17 – ☐ = 10

(b)

10 + 4 = ☐

10 + 1 = ☐

13 – ☐ = 10

(c)

☐ + 2 = 12

☐ + 6 = 16

☐ + 8 = 18

Arrow cards

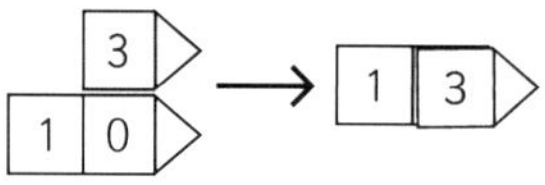

Arrow cards are helpful as different ones cards can be placed over the zero on the tens card. Make a simple set of arrow cards with a longer ten card and nine shorter ones cards. Make the numbers 11 to 19 by placing the ones on top of the ten. Emphasise that the 1 digit in the tens represents 10 for each number. Say, for example that 10 and 4 more is equal to 14.

3.3 Ordering numbers up to 20

Compare and order numbers to 20

1. Join these numbers in the correct order.

19 16 Start 9 12

20 17 10 11 13

18 15 14

2. Two numbers in each set have swapped places. Circle the numbers and write the set in the correct order below.

(a)

14	15	16	18	17	19	20

(b)

8	9	10	13	12	11	14

House numbers

When you are out look at house numbers with your child. Try to find numbers to 20 and look at the next door house number. What does your child notice? If they can see the number 16, for example where do they think number 17 will be?

3.4 Addition and subtraction (1)

Add and subtract using number bonds to 20

1. Complete these number sentences.

(a)

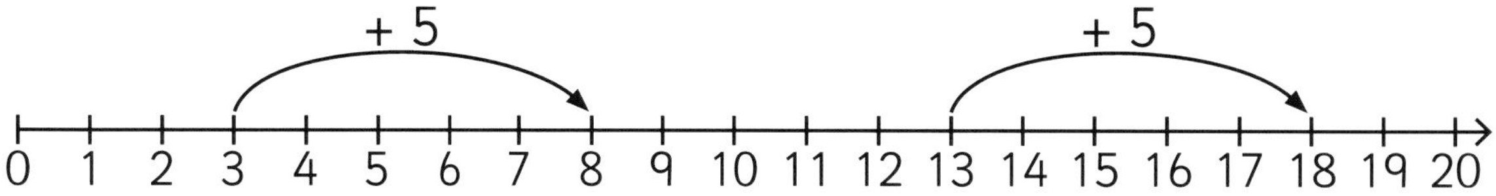

3 (+) 5 = ☐ 13 (+) 5 = ☐

(b)

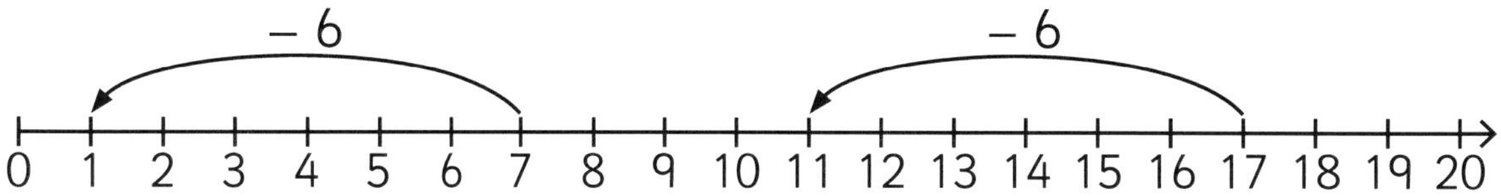

7 (–) 6 = ☐ 17 (–) 6 = ☐

2. Answer these. It might help to draw your own number line.

(a) 4 + 5 = ☐
14 + 5 = ☐

(b) 3 + ☐ = 8
13 + ☐ = 18

(c) ☐ + 2 = 7
☐ + 2 = 17

(d) 7 – 3 = ☐
17 – 3 = ☐

(e) 8 – ☐ = 3
18 – ☐ = 13

(f) ☐ – 4 = 5
☐ – 4 = 15

Ten more

Give your child practise of the number bonds to 10, such as 3 + 4, 5 + 2, 8 + 1, 7 + 2. Tell them that the starting number is going to get bigger by 10, so 13 + 4, 15 + 2, 18 + 1, 17 + 2. Can your child predict that the ones digit will be the same as in the previous answers?

3.5 Addition and subtraction (II) (1)

Add numbers to 20 crossing the ten and partitioning

1. Colour the dots to help answer these. One has been done for you.

(a)

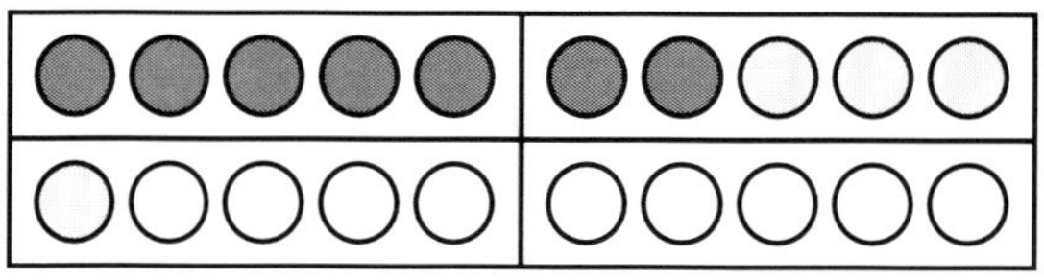

7 + 4 = 11

(b)

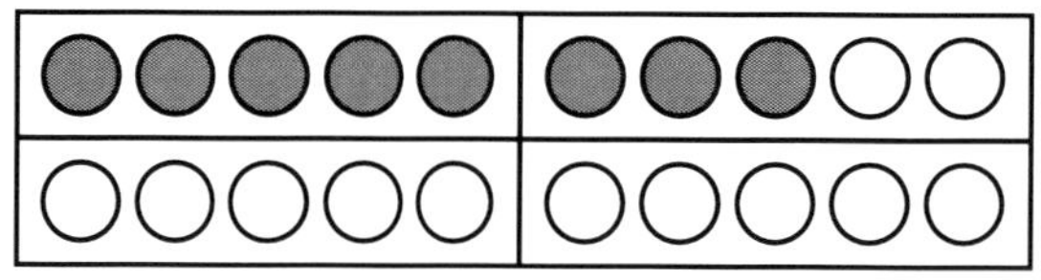

8 + 4 = ☐

(c)

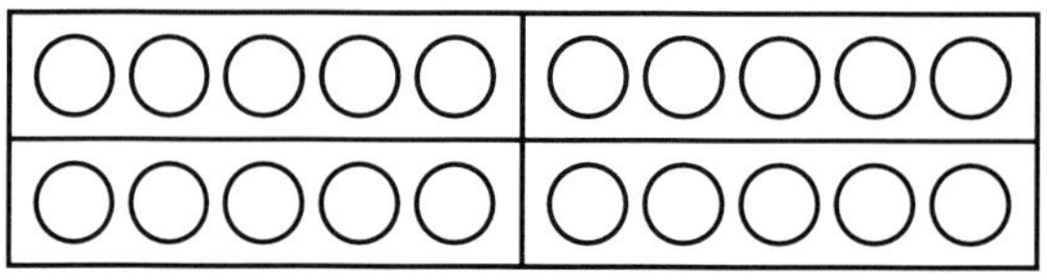

8 + 5 = ☐

(d)

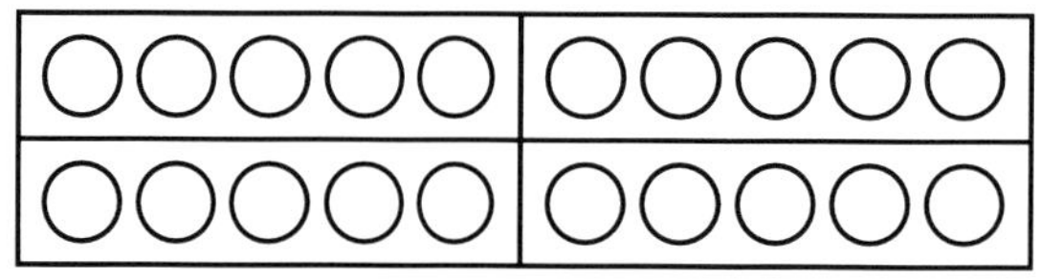

9 + 5 = ☐

2. Write the missing numbers.

(a)

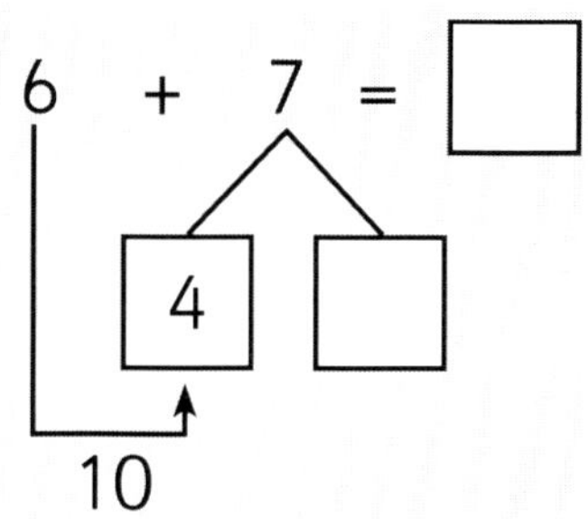

(b)

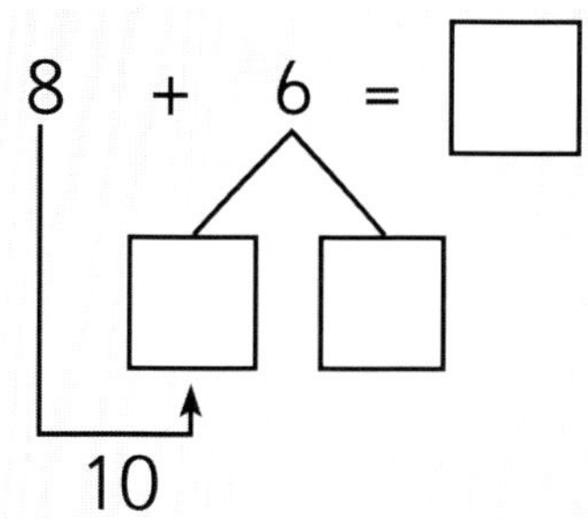

(c)

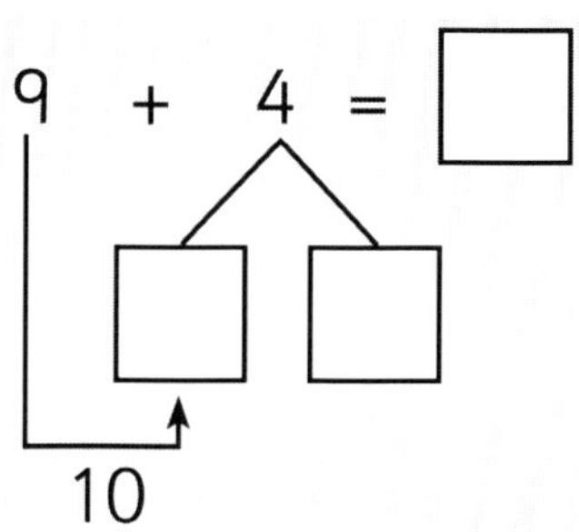

(d)

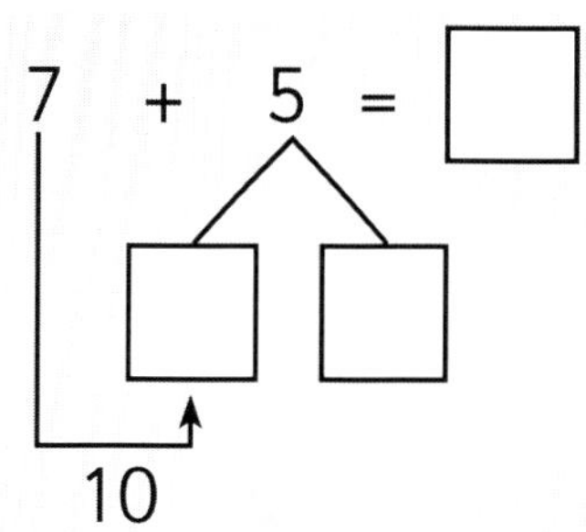

Making 10

For your child to be confident at adding numbers that cross the ten, it helps if they can quickly recall the number bonds for 10: 1 + 9, 2 + 8, 3 + 7, 4 + 6 and 5 + 5. Give your child any number to 10, they say that number and a new number to make a pair of numbers that total 10.

3.6 Addition and subtraction (II) (2)

Add using number bonds to 20 and the commutative law

1. Look at the pictures and write the number sentences.

(a)

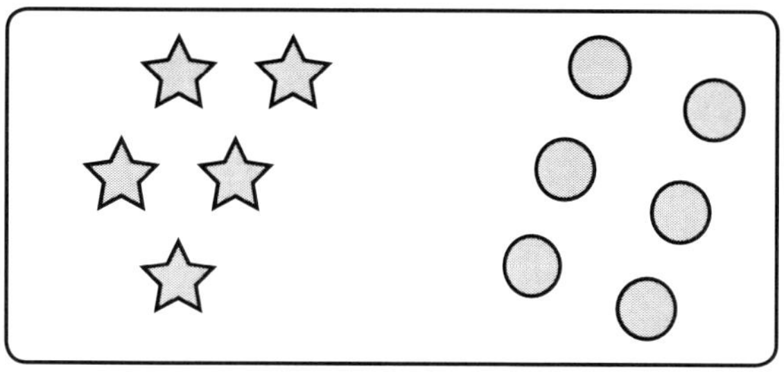

$5 + \square = \square$

$6 + \square = \square$

(b)

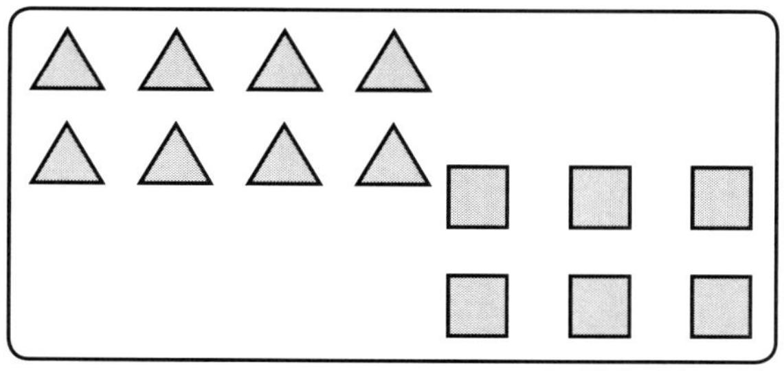

$8 + \square = \square$

$6 + \square = \square$

(c)

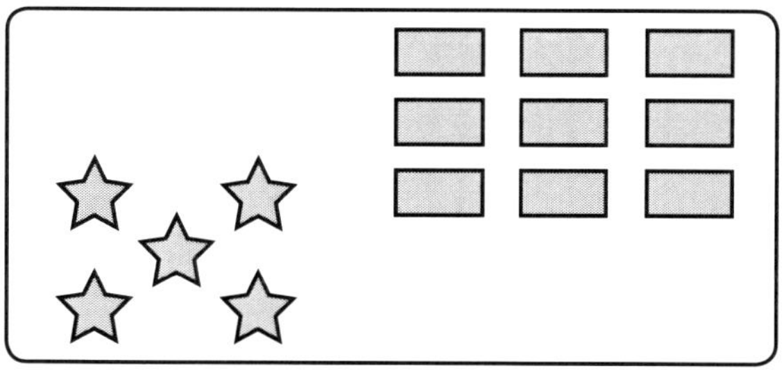

$\square = 9 + \square$

$\square = 5 + \square$

(d)

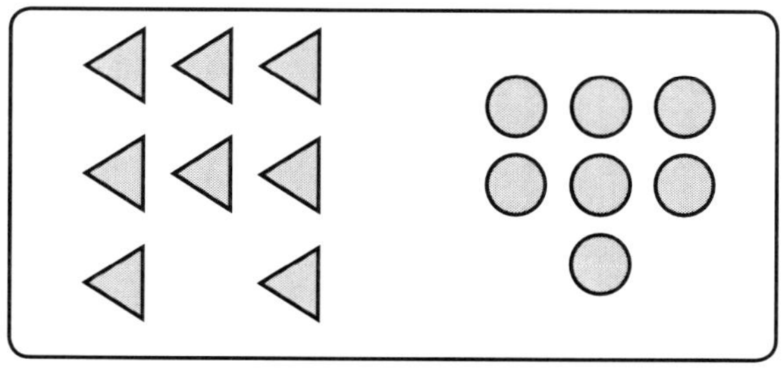

$\square = 8 + \square$

$\square = 7 + \square$

2. Complete these with > , < or =.

(a) 15 ◯ 8 + 4 (b) 9 + 5 ◯ 14 (c) 7 + 8 ◯ 16

(d) 6 + 7 ◯ 12 (e) 19 ◯ 8 + 9 (f) 15 ◯ 6 + 9

Handfuls

Use up to 20 small objects. Ask your child to take a handful in each hand and then choose which hand to count first. They add them together and then try it again, starting with the other handful. Ask them what they notice. Can they explain that the answer will be the same whichever number they start with?

You will need:
20 small objects.

3.7 Addition and subtraction (II) (3)

Subtract within 20, crossing the ten and partitioning

1. Cross out the dots to help answer these.

(a)

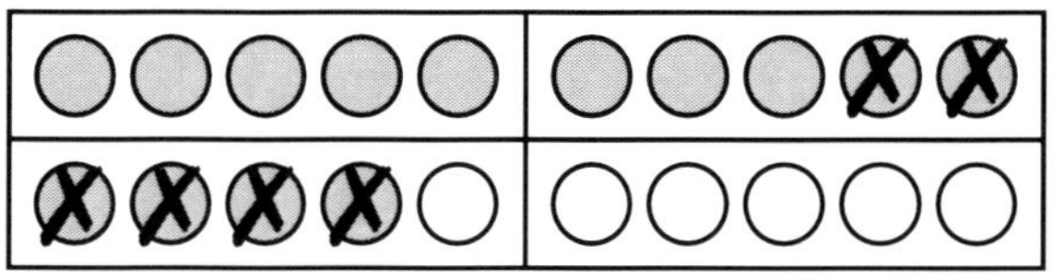

14 − 6 = ☐

(b)

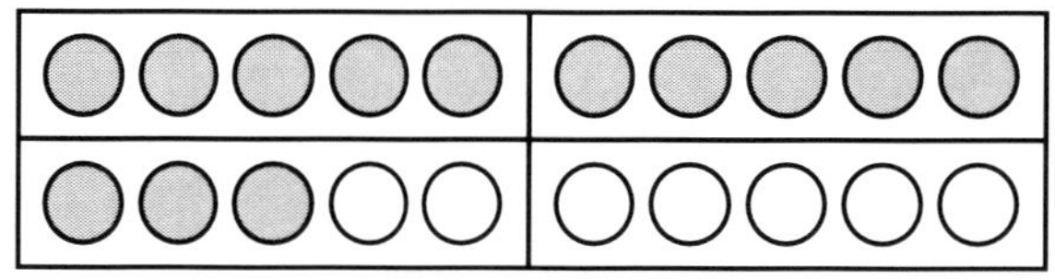

13 − 7 = ☐

(c)

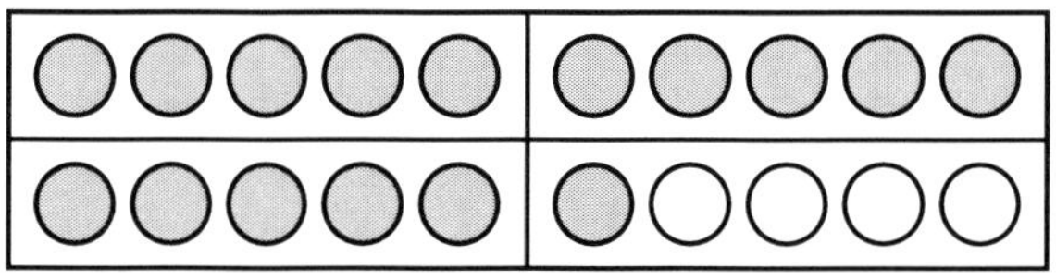

16 − 8 = ☐

(d)

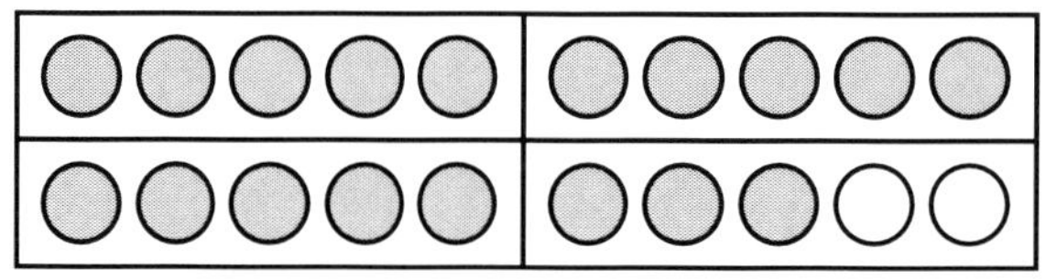

18 − 9 = ☐

2. Write the missing numbers.

(a) 15 − 6 = ☐

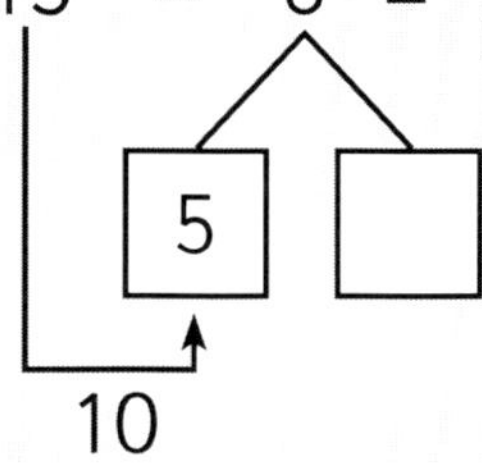

(b) 12 − 7 = ☐

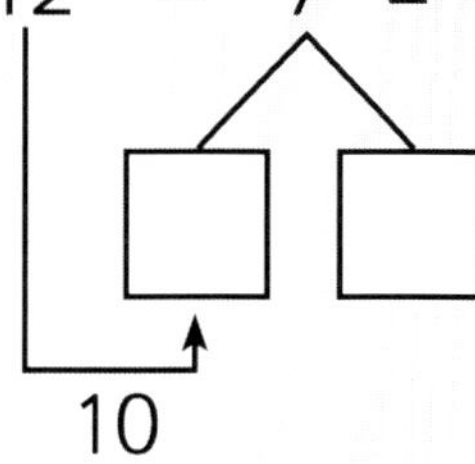

(c) 14 − 8 = ☐

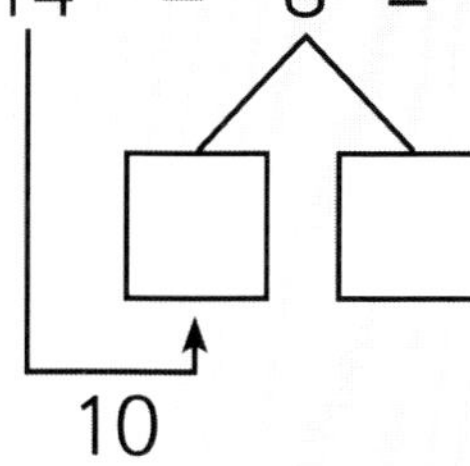

(d) 13 − 5 = ☐

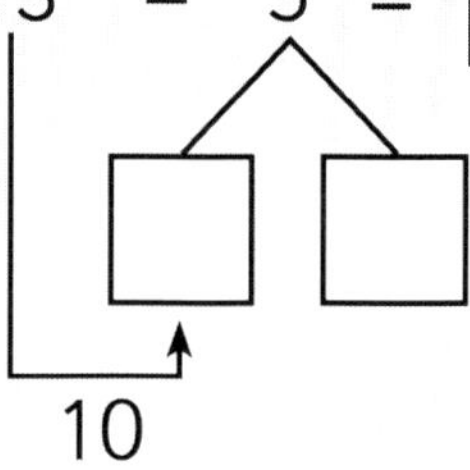

(e) 17 − 8 = ☐

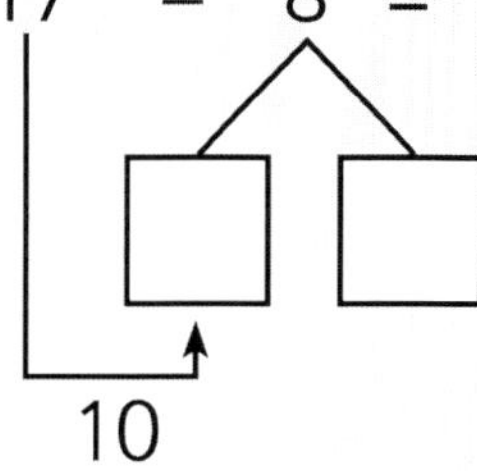

(f) 16 − 9 = ☐

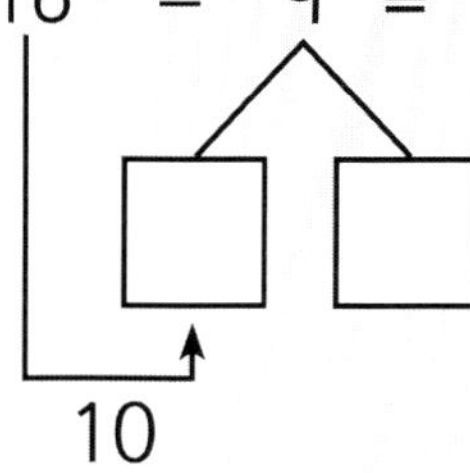

Number line

Counting back on a number line through 10 may help your child subtract numbers. Provide a number line to 20 so they can put a counter on the start number and break up the second number so they land on 10. For example, 15 − 7 will be 15 − 5, then subtract 2.

3.8 Addition and subtraction (II) (4)

Subtract numbers within 20

1. Look at the pictures and write the number sentences.

(a) How many in this box?

There are 11 apples in total.

11 (−) □ = □

(b) How many in this box?

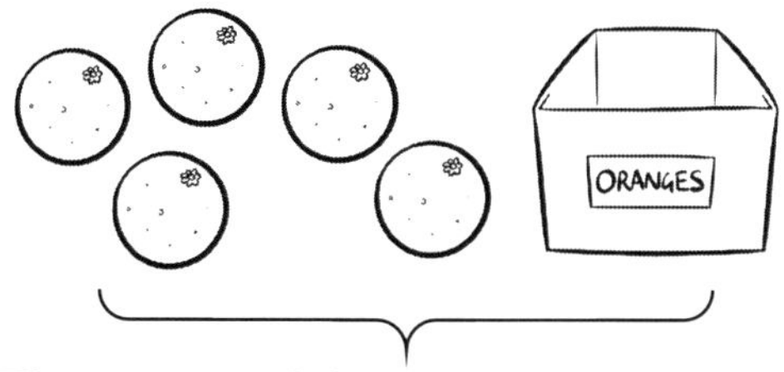

There are 14 oranges in total.

□ ○ □ = □

(c) How many in this bag?

There are 12 lemons in total.

□ ○ □ = □

(d) How many in this bag?

There are 12 bananas in total.

□ ○ □ = □

2. Complete the table.

Minuend	12	11	14	13	15	16
Subtrahend	7	7	9	8	8	9
Difference	5					

New words

Write the subtraction words your child knows on separate pieces of card. Use them to identify different parts of a subtraction calculation. New words include *minuend* – the number being subtracted from and *subtrahend* – the number that is subtracted to leave the *difference*. They also know about the *whole* being made up of *parts* – so the whole is the same as the minuend and the parts are the same as the subtrahend and the difference.

3.9 Addition and subtraction (II) (5)

Add and subtract numbers to 20

1. Look at the pictures and write the number sentences.

(a) How many cars are there in total?

□ ○ □ = □

(b) How many bikes are there in total?

□ ○ □ = □

2. Join these to the matching answers.

(a) 7 + 6

(b) 16 – 7

(c) 11 – 4

(d) 7 + 4

(e) 6 + 5

(f) 14 – 7

(g) 12 – 3

(h) 9 + 4

7

9

11

13

Shopping

When shopping in a supermarket with your child, take the opportunity to add and subtract. Ask how many tins there are altogether in your basket and how many there would be if three were put back on the shelf. Ask how many tomatoes, for example in a pack and how many in total if you bought four more or two packs.

3.10 Let's talk and calculate (III)

Interpret word problems using addition and subtraction facts to 20

1. Read these and write the addition or subtraction sentences.

(a) There are 5 books on a shelf. 6 more books are added. How many are on the shelf now?

☐ ◯ ☐ = ☐

(b) 12 cakes are on a plate. 3 cakes are eaten. How many cakes are left on the plate?

☐ ◯ ☐ = ☐

2. Answer these. Draw pictures to help you.

a) 9 ducks were swimming in a pond. Some more ducks flew onto the pond. There were now 12 ducks. How many ducks flew onto the pond? ☐

b) Sam had 12 sweets. He ate some of the sweets and had 8 left. How many sweets did he eat? ☐

Drawing pictures

Give your child addition and subtraction stories like the ones above and encourage your child to draw a picture to show the story. This will help them 'act out' the problem and make sense of the calculation – whether to add or subtract.

3.11 Adding on and taking away

Use the inverse relationship between addition and subtraction with numbers to 20

1. Look at the picture and fill in the boxes.

(a)

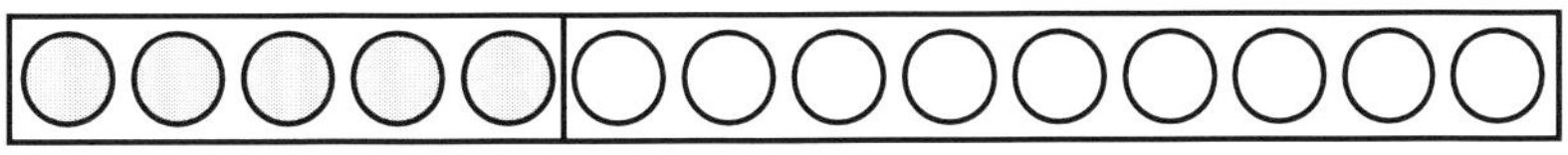

5 + 9 = ☐

14 – 9 = ☐

(b)

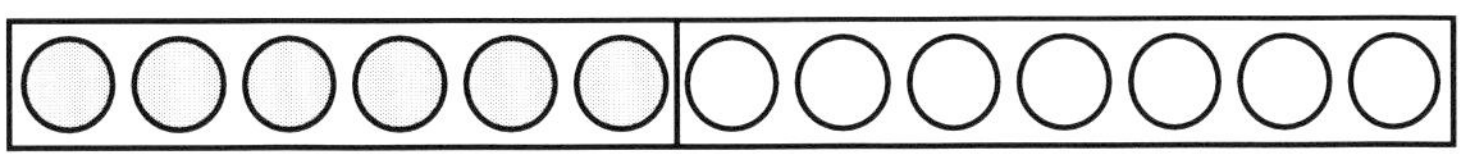

6 + ☐ = ☐

☐ – ☐ = ☐

2. Complete these. Use the number line to help.

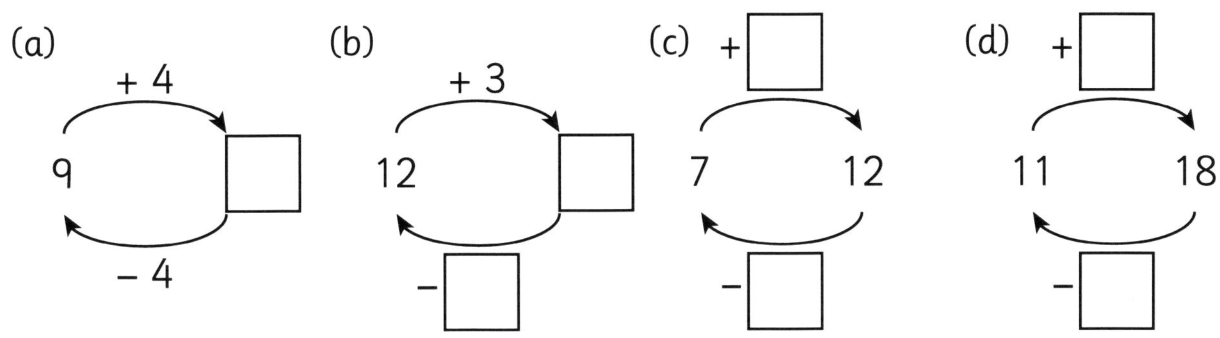

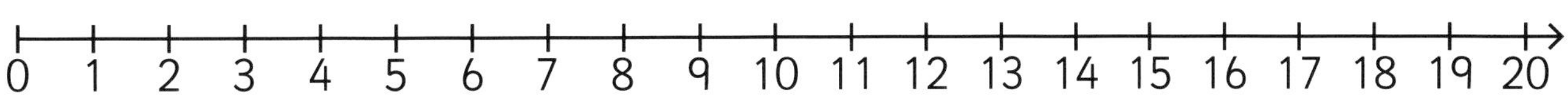

Three numbers

Give three numbers from an addition sentence with a total less than 20, for example 4, 15 and 19. Work with your child to find the four facts for these: 4 + 15 = 19, 15 + 4 = 19, 19 – 15 = 4, 19 – 4 = 15. Repeat with two other sets of numbers.

3.12 Number walls

Use the number bonds to 20

1. Complete these number walls. One has been done for you.

(a)

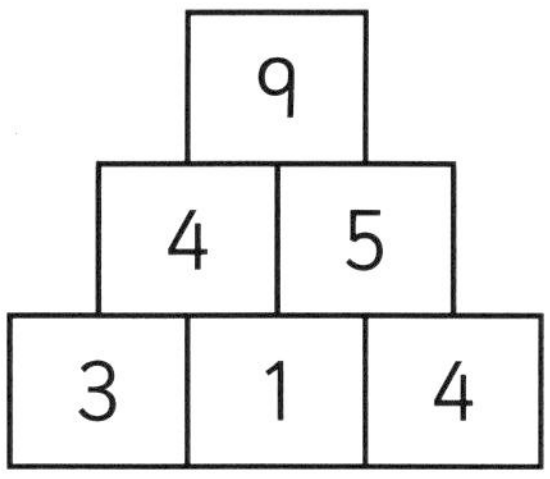

(b)

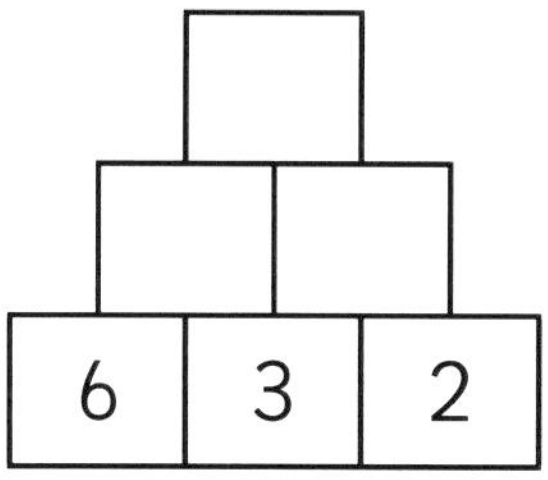

(c)

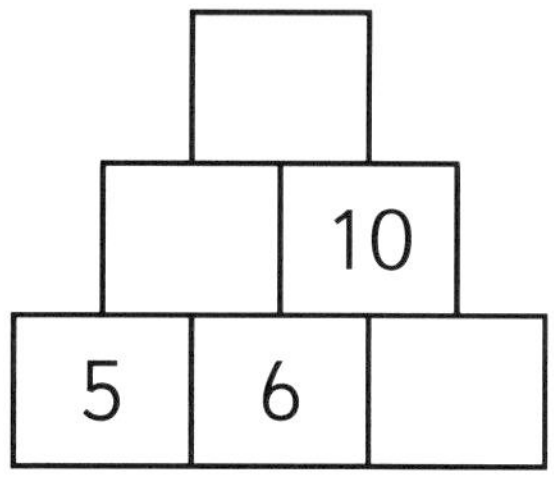

(d)

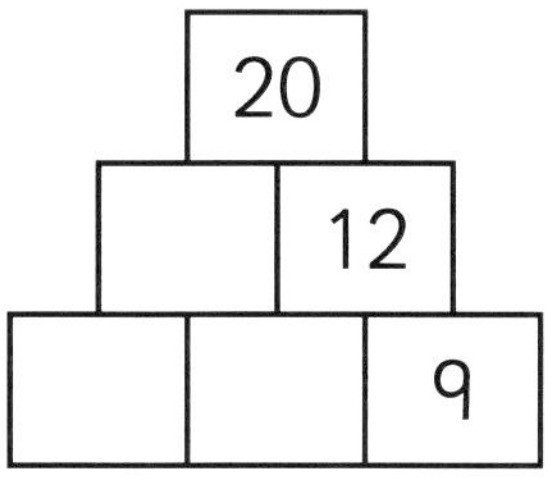

(e)

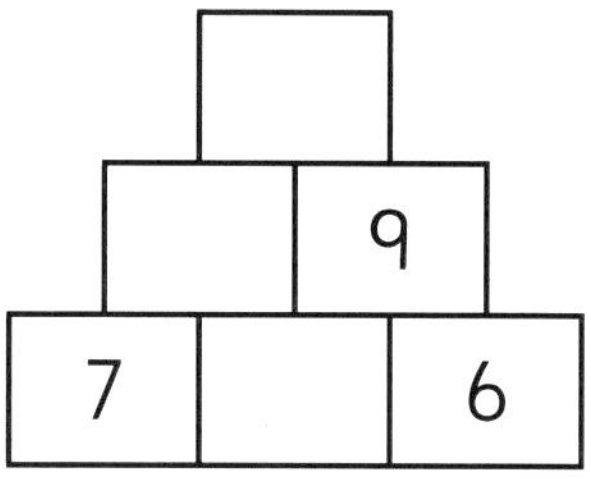

(f)

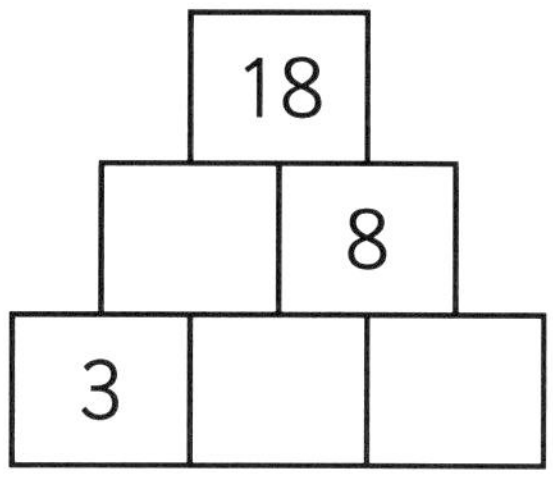

2. Now try these.

(a)

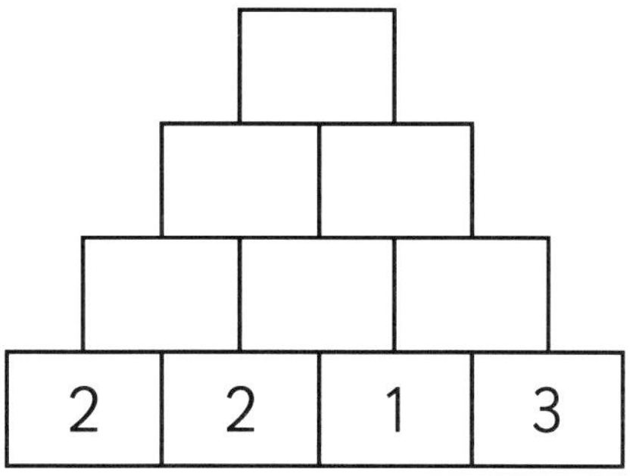

(b)

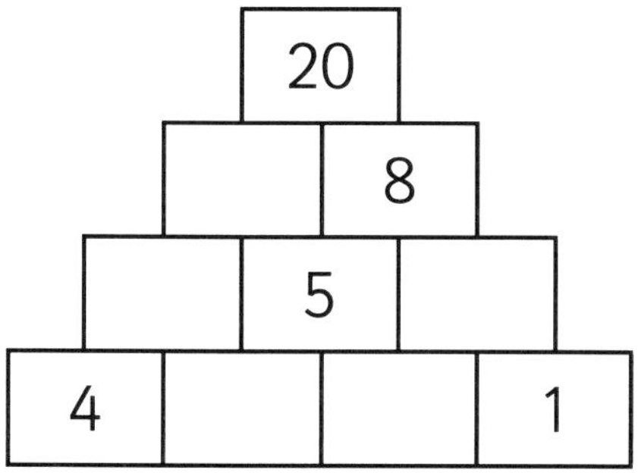

3. Make your own number walls. Make each one different.

(a)

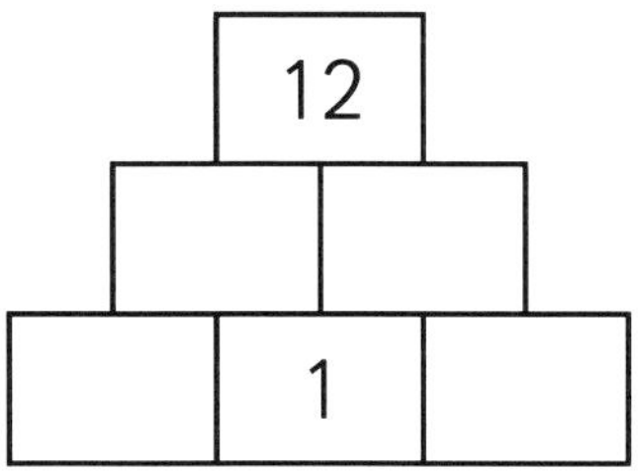

(b)

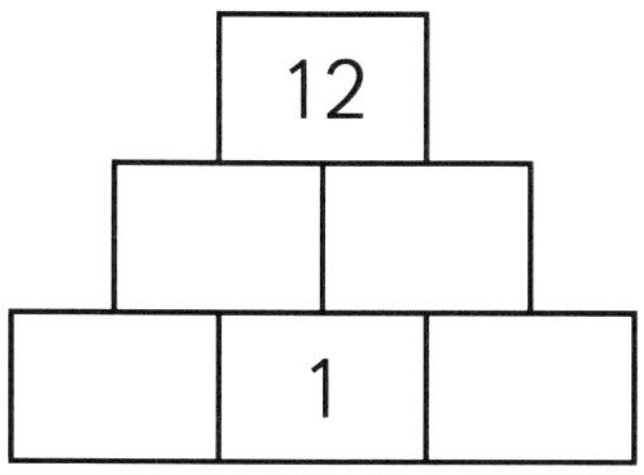

Making 20

Give your child some blank '3 row' number walls. Write the number 20 in the top square and ask your child to find two different ways to complete the number wall.

4.1 Shapes of objects (1)

Recognise and name 3-D shapes

1. Join the matching shapes.

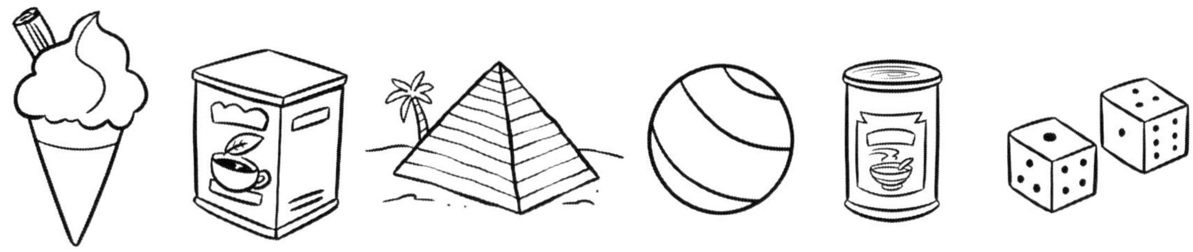

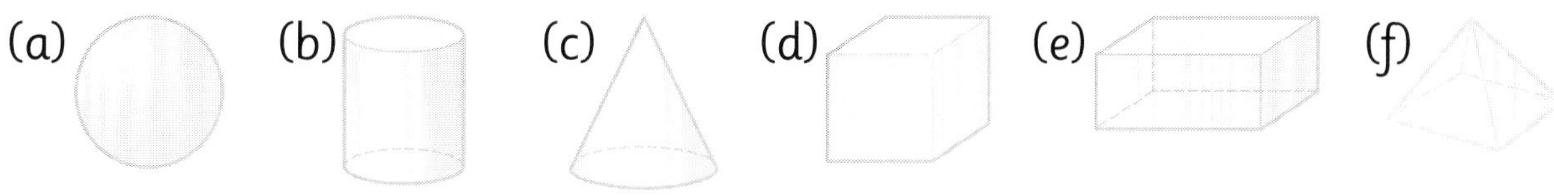

2. Count the shapes on the shelves. Write the number.

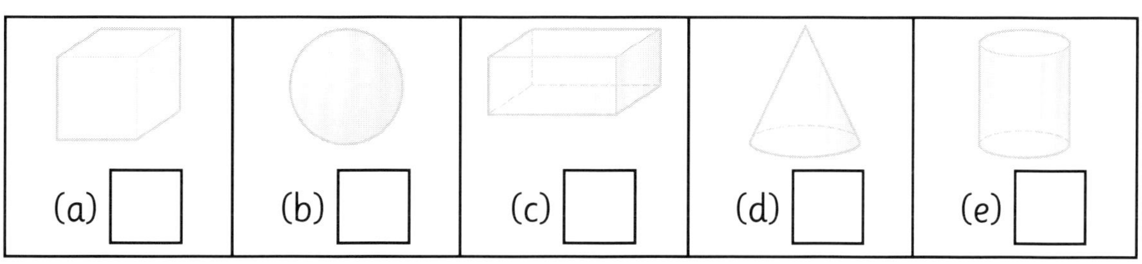

Shape match

Your child will be able to show you an edge, a face and a vertex on simple 3-D shapes around the home. Ask your child to find pairs of shapes that are the same, for example a box and a book are both cuboids, a pencil and tin of beans are both cylinders.

4.2 Shapes of objects (2)

Recognise and name 3-D shapes

1. Circle the odd one out in each set.

a) 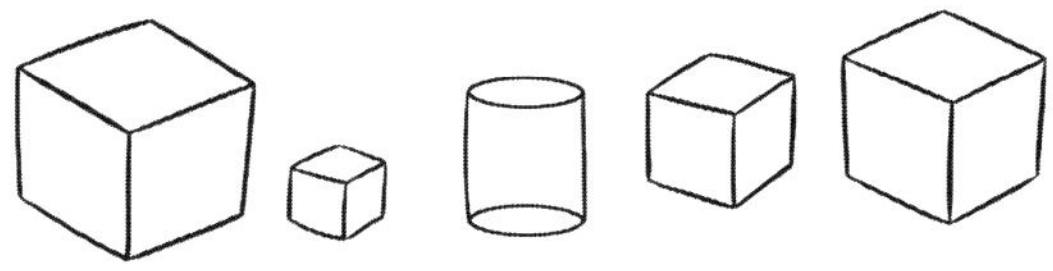

b) 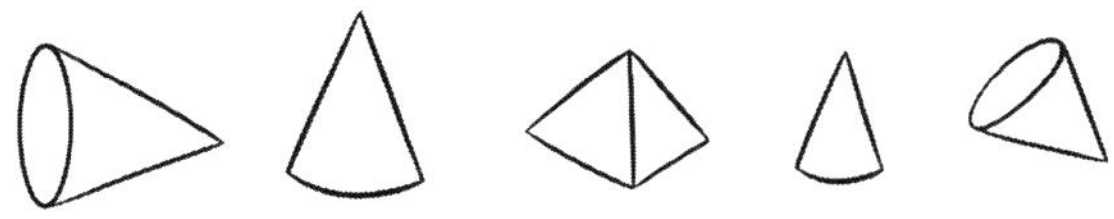

c) 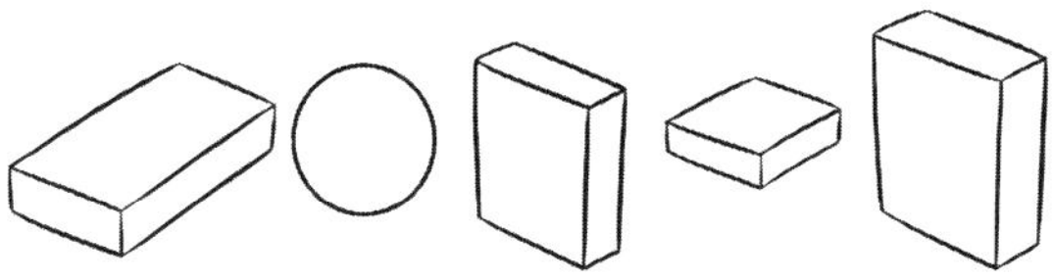

d) 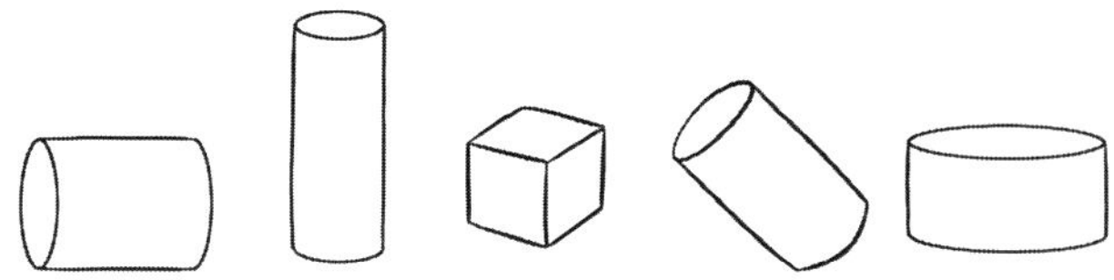

e) 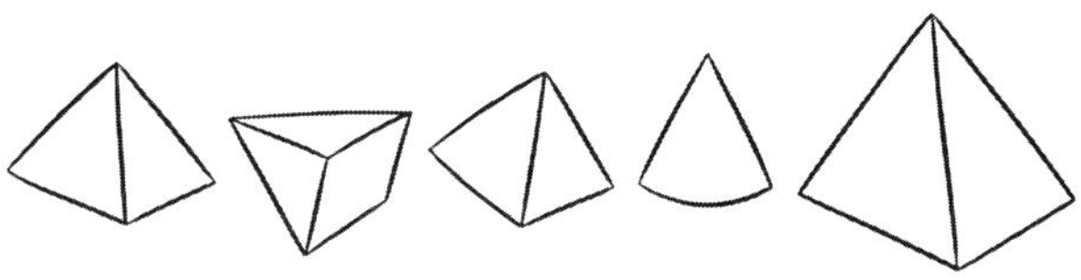

2. Draw a line to match each lid to the correct box.

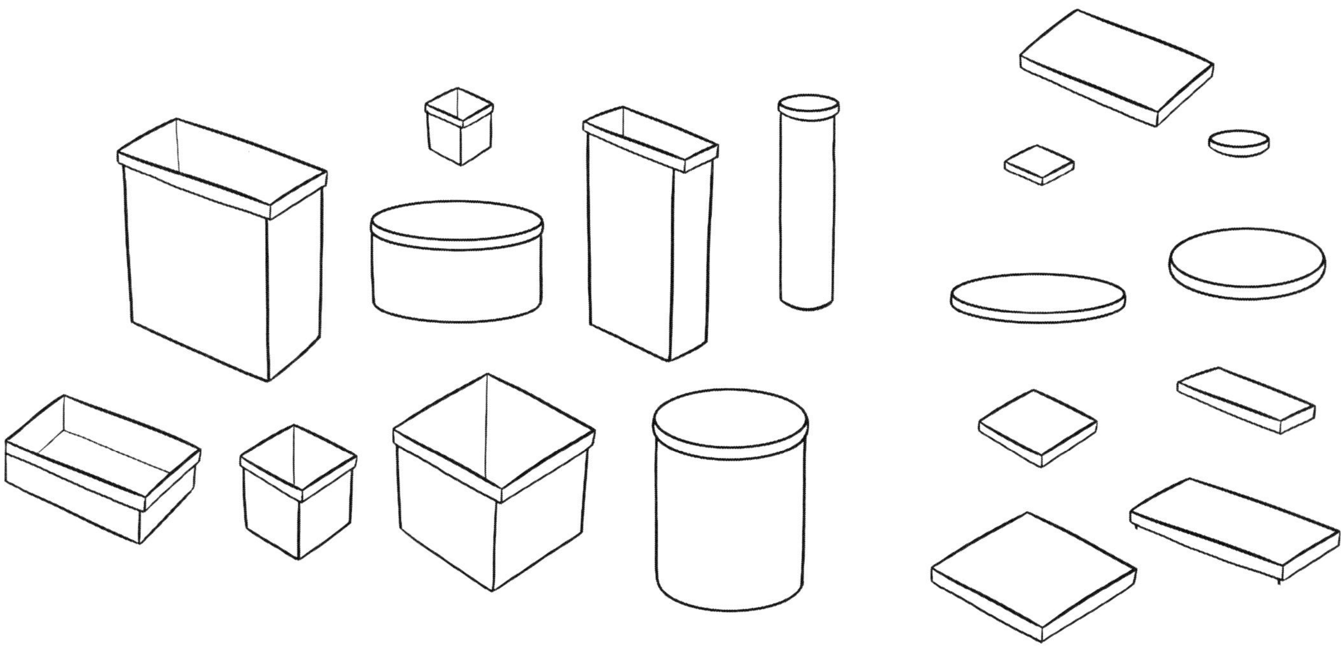

Packets of biscuits

With your child, look at the shapes of biscuits you have at home. The most usual shapes are circles, squares and rectangles. Compare the shapes and talk about the way they are the same as, or different from, each other. Now look at the packets they are in. The stacked biscuits could make cylinders, cubes or cuboids and you can compare the faces of the individual biscuits.

5.1 Sorting shapes

Recognise and sort 2-D shapes

1. Look for ◯ circles, □ squares and ▭ rectangles.
Colour and count the shapes.

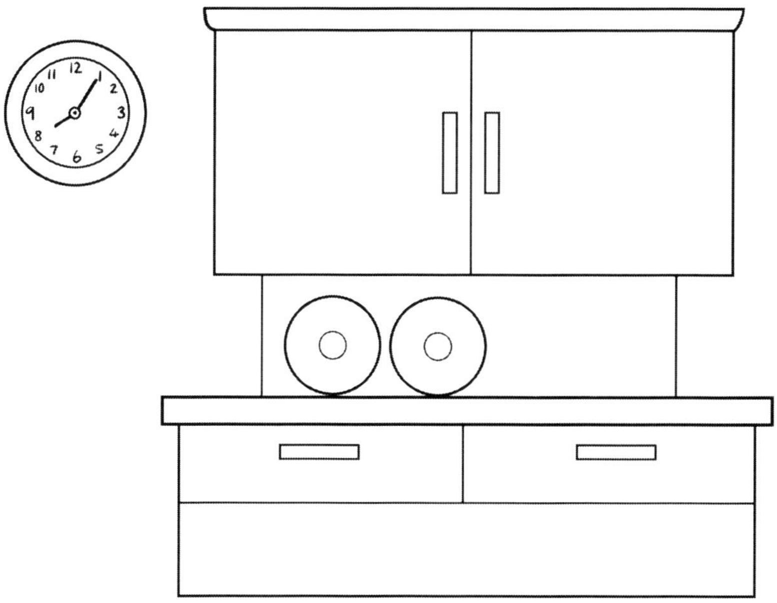

	How many?
(a) ◯ red	
(b) □ blue	
(c) ▭ green	

2. Sort these shapes. Draw a line to show where they belong.

	square □	circle ◯	rectangle ▭
small			
large			

How many △ triangles are left? □

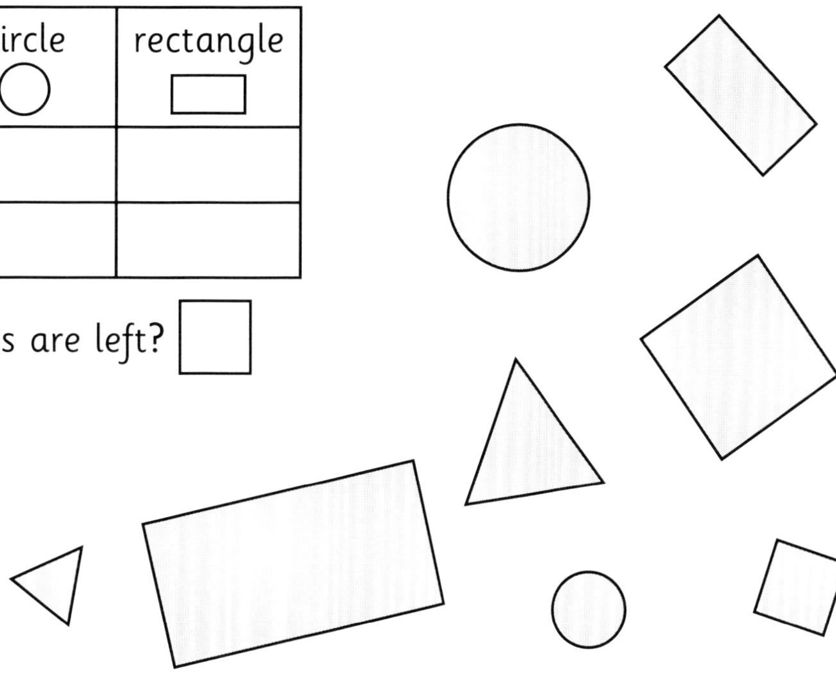

Shape hunt

Choose a shape: square, circle, rectangle or triangle and ask your child to draw the chosen shape on a piece of paper. Go on a shape hunt around the house. When you find a shape ask what is the same and what is different about the shape compared to the shape drawn. Talk about number of sides and corners.

5.2 Calculating with reasoning

Add and subtract numbers to 20

1. Fill in the boxes.

IN ▷ +5 ◁ OUT

	IN	OUT
(a)	12	
(b)	11	
(c)	10	
(d)	9	
(e)	8	

IN ▷ +6 ◁ OUT

	IN	OUT
(f)	5	
(g)	6	
(h)	7	
(i)	8	
(j)	9	

IN ▷ +7 ◁ OUT

	IN	OUT
(k)	8	
(l)	9	
(m)	10	
(n)	11	
(o)	12	

2. Answer these.

(a) $17 - 7 = \square$

(b) $17 - 8 = \square$

(c) $17 - 9 = \square$

(d) $15 - 5 = \square$

(e) $14 - 5 = \square$

(f) $13 - 5 = \square$

(g) $14 - 7 = \square$

(h) $15 - 8 = \square$

(i) $16 - 9 = \square$

3. Colour the cloud with a different answer to the others in each set.

(a) $14 - 6$ $9 - 2$ $15 - 8$ $12 - 5$ $11 - 4$

(b) $12 + 3$ $9 + 6$ $11 + 4$ $8 + 7$ $5 + 9$

Adding machine

You will need:
a cardboard box.

Make a function machine from a cardboard box. Put an 'IN' and 'OUT' slot on opposite sides and write the numbers 0–15 on pieces of card. Write +5 on the front to make it an 'add five' machine. Put in a number on a piece of card through the IN slot and ask your child what number will come out. Repeat with other numbers.

5.3 Comparing numbers

Compare numbers to 20

1. Draw and complete these.

a) Draw 2 more ☐ than ☆.

Total ☐

Total ☐

b) Draw 3 fewer ◯ than ▭.

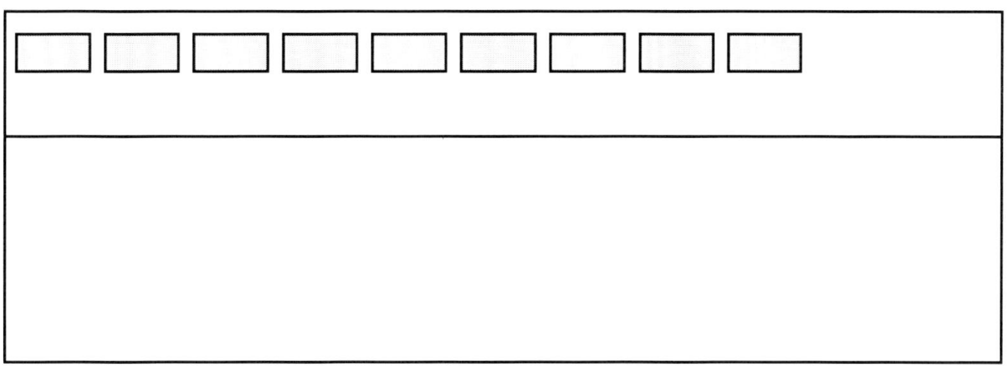

Total ☐

Total ☐

2. Compare these and write >, < or =.

(a) 16 ◯ 14

(b) 13 ◯ 15

(c) 19 ◯ 20

(d) 9 + 4 ◯ 13

(e) 17 – 6 ◯ 10

(f) 4 + 7 ◯ 9

(g) 3 + 7 ◯ 20 – 5

(h) 11 – 3 ◯ 14 – 7

(i) 12 – 3 ◯ 6 + 5

Balancing

Make card signs for less than <, greater than > and equals =. Put them on a table with a handful of counters or buttons on either side of one of the signs. Ask your child to add or subtract to either side to make some number sentences so that the symbol between the piles of items is true. Repeat a few times.

You will need: small objects for counting.

5.4 Half and quarter

Recognise a half and a quarter of shapes and quantities

1. Tick (✓) the shapes that have been halved.

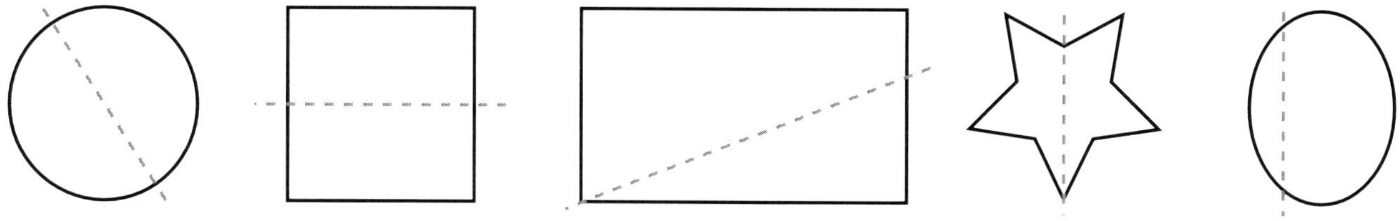

(a) ☐ (b) ☐ (c) ☐ (d) ☐ (e) ☐

2. Colour a quarter of each of these shapes.

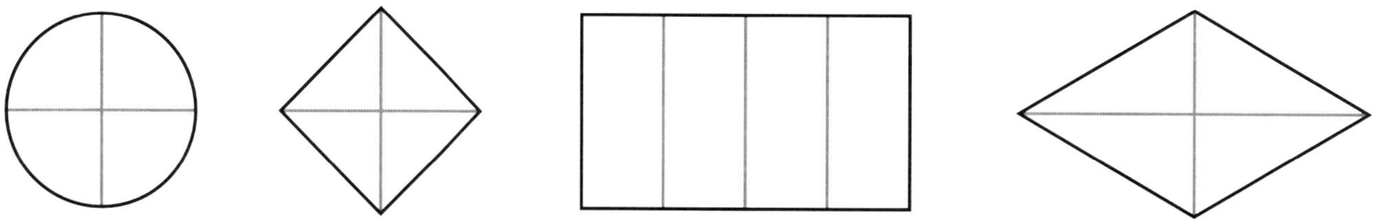

3. Colour half the dots and write the number sentences.

(a) ○○○○ ○○○○

☐ + ☐ = ☐

(b) ○○○○○ ○○○○○

☐ + ☐ = ☐

(c) ○○○○○○ ○○○○○○

☐ + ☐ = ☐

4. Complete these.

(a) 6 —double→ ☐

(b) ☐ —double→ 14

(c) 16 —half→ ☐

(d) ☐ —half→ 9

Slicing food

Encourage your child to recognise half and quarter at the table. Cut different things: a pizza, orange, apple, slice of bread or cake into halves and ask is this half or quarter? Cut again to make quarters and ask again, is this quarter or half? Let your child cut their own modelling clay foods into halves and quarters.

5.5 Let's do additions together

Use number bonds to 20

1. Join each kite to the matching answer.

5 + 6 | 7 + 8 | 8 + 5 | 7 + 10 | 6 + 9 | 4 + 9 | 8 + 3 | 9 + 8

(a) 11 (b) 13 (c) 15 (d) 17

2. Write the missing numbers. The top number is the answer for each addition below.

12

(a) 2 + 10
(b) 3 + □
(c) 4 + □
(d) 5 + □
(e) 6 + □

14

(f) □ + 10
(g) □ + 9
(h) □ + □
(i) □ + □
(j) □ + □

16

(k) 6 + □
(l) 7 + □
(m) □ + □
(n) □ + □
(o) □ + □

Addition problems

Ask your child to make up some addition problems. Write a number sentence, for example 7 + 4 = 11 and then your child can make up a problem, such as: *I have 7 crayons and 4 pens, so I have 11 crayons and pens in my pencil case.* As a challenge make one of the numbers an empty box, for example □ + 4 = 11.

5.6 Let's do subtraction together

Use number bonds to subtract numbers within 20

1. Join each car to the matching answer.

2. Write the missing numbers.

7	8	9
(a) 17 – 10	(f) ☐ – 3	(k) 10 – ☐
(b) 16 – ☐	(g) ☐ – 4	(l) 11 – ☐
(c) 15 – ☐	(h) ☐ – ☐	(m) ☐ – ☐
(d) 14 – ☐	(i) ☐ – ☐	(n) ☐ – ☐
(e) 13 – ☐	(j) ☐ – ☐	(o) ☐ – ☐

3. There are 14 green and red apples in a box.
8 of the apples are red. How many are green? ☐

Write the complete number sentence.

____

Subtraction problems

Ask your child to make up subtraction problems. Write a number sentence, for example 15 – 9 = 6 and then your child can make up a problem, such as: *I have 15 stickers, I use 9 of them and I have 6 stickers left*. As a challenge make one of the numbers an empty box, for example 15 – ☐ = 6.

5.7 Making number sentences

Make addition and subtraction sentences using the inverse relationship

1. Look at the pictures and write the number sentences.

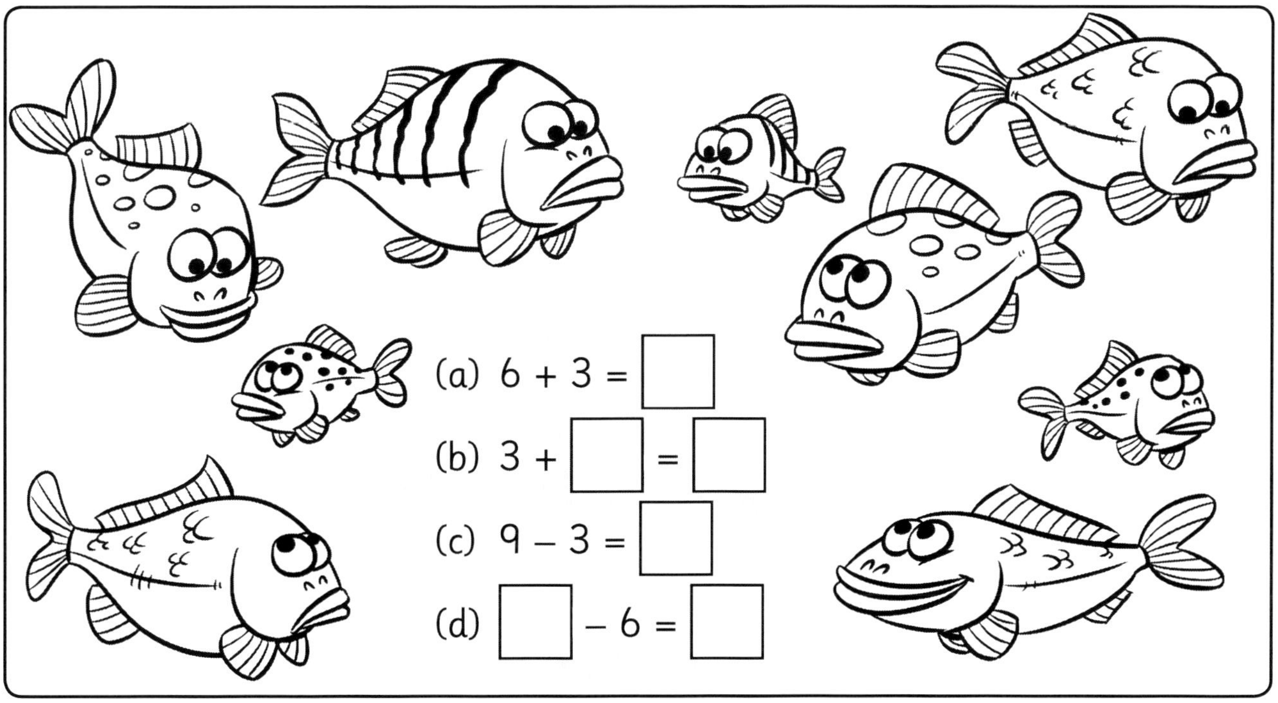

(a) $6 + 3 = \square$

(b) $3 + \square = \square$

(c) $9 - 3 = \square$

(d) $\square - 6 = \square$

2. Complete the additions and subtractions for each of these.

(a)

14	
8	6

$\square + \square = \square$

$\square + \square = \square$

$\square - \square = \square$

$\square - \square = \square$

(b)

12	
7	5

$\square + \square = \square$

$\square + \square = \square$

$\square - \square = \square$

$\square - \square = \square$

Splitting towers

Use interlocking cubes or bricks of two colours. Ask your child to make a tower to show 4 + 5 = 9. They then split the tower of 9 cubes to show 9 – 4, 9 – 5 and then 5 + 4. Repeat for other totals up to 20.

You will need:
interlocking cubes or bricks.

5.8 Mathematics playground (1)

Read, write, add and subtract numbers to 20

1. Look carefully at these number patterns.
Write the missing numbers.

(a)

11			14			17	

(b)

6	8			14			20

(c)

3		7		11	13		

2. Write <, > or = in the ◯.

(a) 8 + 2 ◯ 12

(b) 9 – 4 ◯ 3

(c) 7 + 9 ◯ 16

(d) 15 ◯ 7 + 8

(e) 13 ◯ 18 – 7

(f) 14 ◯ 19 – 6

(g) 6 + 3 ◯ 5 + 5

(h) 9 – 5 ◯ 12 – 8

(i) 7 + 2 ◯ 13 – 5

3. Look at the picture and write the number sentences.

(a) 6 + ☐ = 14

(b) ☐ + 6 = ☐

(c) 14 – ☐ = 6

(d) ☐ – ☐ = 8

Number chains

Don't forget to keep practising adding and subtracting with numbers to 10. Play 'number chains' with your child. Start with any number and add or subtract small numbers to keep it under 10. For example, **3** add 4 → **7** take away 2 → **5** take away 1 → **4** add 5 → 9.

5.9 Mathematics playground (2)

Add and subtract numbers to 20

1. Write additions and subtractions for these signposts.

(a)

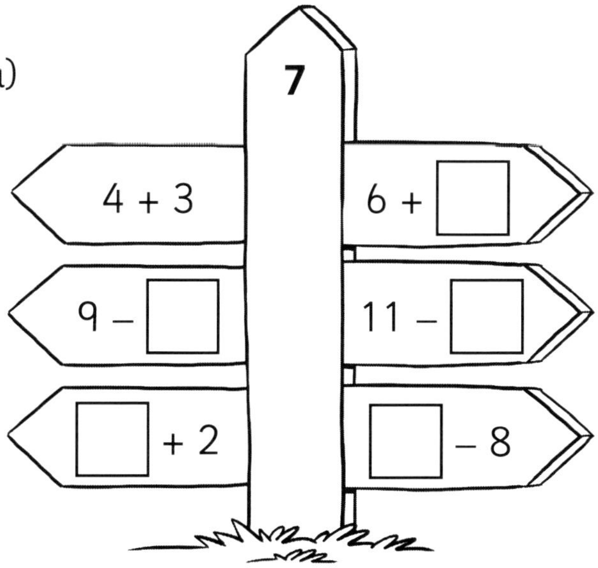

(b)

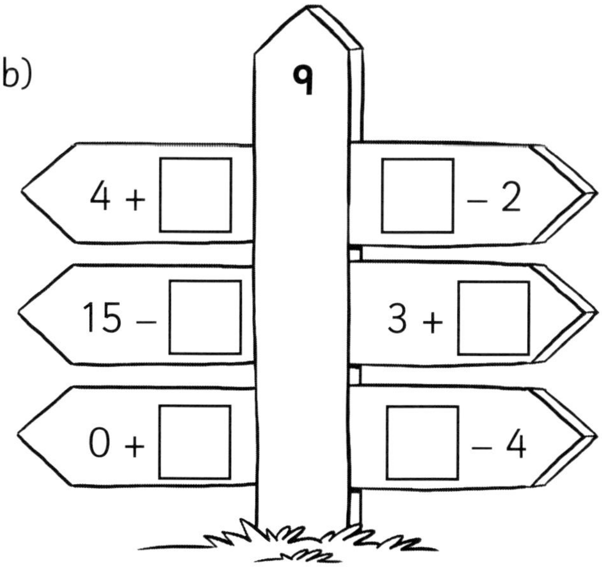

2. Write addition and subtraction facts from the ones given.

4 + 9 = 13	8 + 5 = 13	7 + 6 = 13
(a) 9 + □ = 13	(d) □ + 8 = □	(g) 6 + □ = □
(b) □ – 9 = □	(e) □ – □ = 8	(h) □ – □ = 6
(c) □ – □ = 9	(f) □ – 8 = □	(i) □ – 6 = □

Trio cards

Make a set of 'trio' cards for your child to use. Write number bonds up to 20 in the corners of each triangle, with the total at the top, for example:

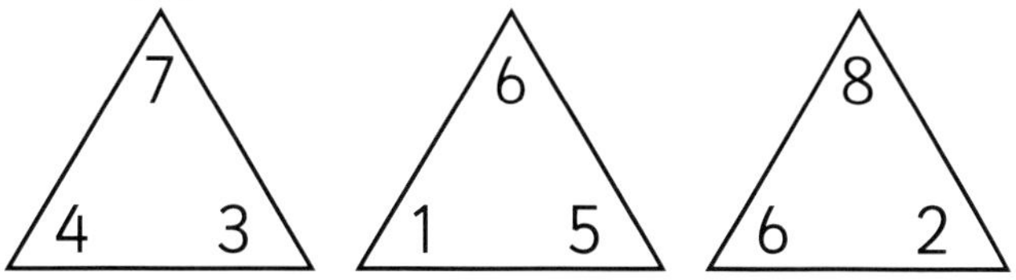

Take one trio at a time and cover one of the numbers in a corner with your thumb. Your child tries to work out the missing number, for example 4 + 3 = □, 7 – 3 = □ or 7 – 4 = □.

5.10 Mathematics playground (3)

Use number bonds to add and subtract numbers to 20

1. Complete the number track.

10 + 1	10 + 2	10 + 3			10 + 6				
11			14	15					

2. Write the numbers coming out of these machines.

IN → +6 → OUT

	IN	OUT
(a)	4	
(b)	5	
(c)	6	
(d)	7	
(e)	8	
(f)		

IN → −6 → OUT

	IN	OUT
(g)	10	
(h)	11	
(i)	12	
(j)	13	
(k)	14	
(l)		

Number machines

Use the number machines you made previously, or make one from a cardboard box. Give the box a rule, such as 'Subtract 4' and change the starting number and the number subtracted so your child can work out the number coming out of the machine. Ask your child what would happen if the number that came out went back through the machine. This shows that addition is the inverse of subtraction.

You will need:
a cardboard box.

6.1 Tens and ones

Partition numbers to 100 into tens and ones

1. Count and complete these.

(a)

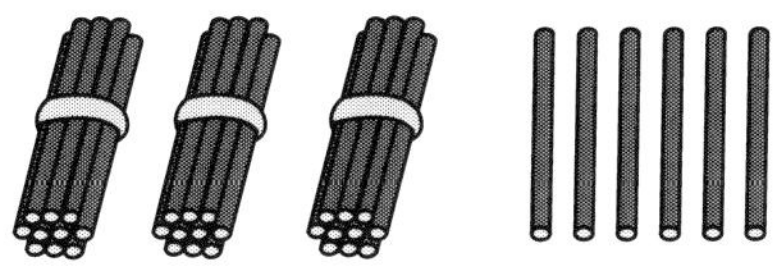

3 tens and ___ ones

equals ___

30 + ___ = ___

(b)

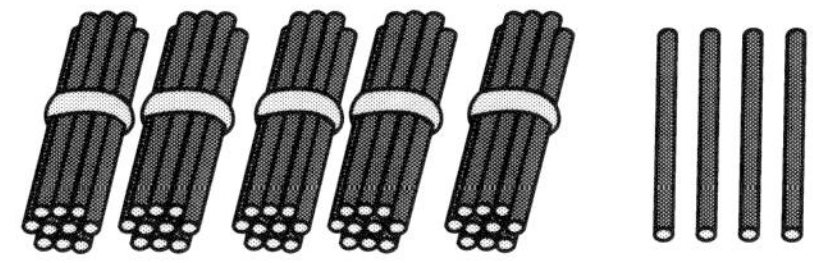

___ tens and ___ ones

equals ___

___ + ___ = ___

(c)

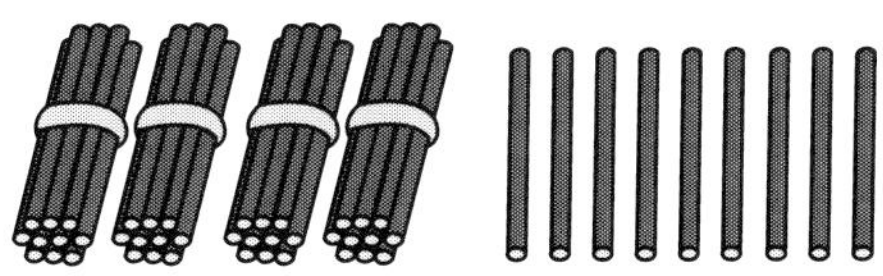

___ tens and ___ ones

equals ___

___ + ___ = ___

(d)

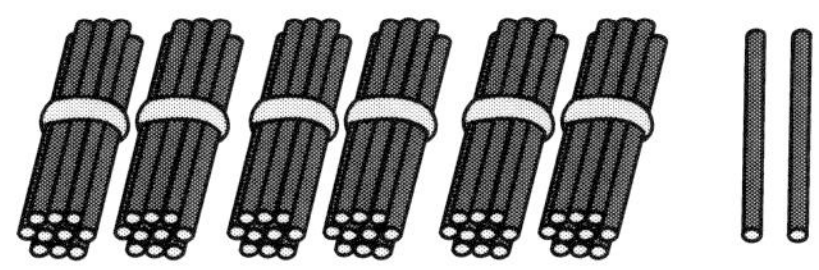

___ tens and ___ ones

equals ___

___ + ___ = ___

2. Write the numbers.

(a) 3 0 + 4 = ___ ___

(b) 5 0 + 6 = ___ ___

(c) ___ ___ = 4 0 + 3

(d) ___ ___ = 6 0 + 5

Arrow cards

Use the arrow cards you have made (see page 32 to make a new set) and make new tens cards 20 to 90. Make different two-digit numbers, breaking them up to see that, for example 45 is 40 + 5. Try and make pairs with the same digits but with different values. Talk about how they are different. For example, 25 and 52 or 83 and 38.

6.2 Knowing 100

Add tens to total 100 and subtract tens from 100

1. Write the missing numbers to complete the number line.

0	10		30				70			

2. Use the diagram to complete these.

1	2	3	4	5	6	7	8	9	10
11	12	13	14	15	16	17	18	19	20
21	22	23	24	25	26	27	28	29	30
31	32	33	34	35	36	37	38	39	40
41	42	43	44	45	46	47	48	49	50
51	52	53	54	55	56	57	58	59	60
61	62	63	64	65	66	67	68	69	70
71	72	73	74	75	76	77	78	79	80
81	82	83	84	85	86	87	88	89	90
91	92	93	94	95	96	97	98	99	100

(a) 50 + 10 = ☐

(b) 50 + 20 = ☐

(c) 50 + 30 = ☐

(d) 50 + 40 = ☐

(e) 50 + 50 = ☐

(f) 90 – 60 = ☐

(g) 80 – 50 = ☐

(h) 70 – 40 = ☐

(i) 60 – 30 = ☐

(j) 50 – 20 = ☐

(k) 80 + ☐ = 90

(l) 70 + ☐ = 90

(m) 60 + ☐ = 90

(n) 50 + ☐ = 90

(o) 40 + ☐ = 90

(p) ☐ – 10 = 30

(q) ☐ – 20 = 30

(r) ☐ – 30 = 30

(s) ☐ – 40 = 30

(t) ☐ – 50 = 30

Making 100

Use the tens arrow cards from the set your made previously or make a new set (see page 32). Lay them face down and take turns with your child to turn over cards one at a time to find pairs that make 100. The game is over once there is only one card, 50, left on the table. Count the pairs making 100 for each player, the player with the most wins.

6.3 Representing numbers up to 100 (1)

Recognise the place value of 2-digit numbers

1. Count the dots and write the numbers.

(a)

Tens	Ones
●●● ●●●	

→ ☐

(b)

Tens	Ones
●●●● ●●●	

→ ☐

(c)

Tens	Ones
●●●● ●●●●	

→ ☐

(d)

Tens	Ones
●●● ●●	

→ ☐

2. Draw the dots and write the numbers.

(a) 30 + 4 = ☐

Tens	Ones

(b) 50 + 6 = ☐

Tens	Ones

(c) 40 + 7 = ☐

Tens	Ones

(d) 60 + 5 = ☐

Tens	Ones

Numbers all around

As you walk past houses or go shopping, ask your child to spot any two-digit numbers they can see. Encourage them to say the number and then break it up into tens and ones, for example 34 is 30 and 4.

6.4 Representing numbers up to 100 (2)

Recognise and compare numbers to 100

1. Join these to their position on the number line.

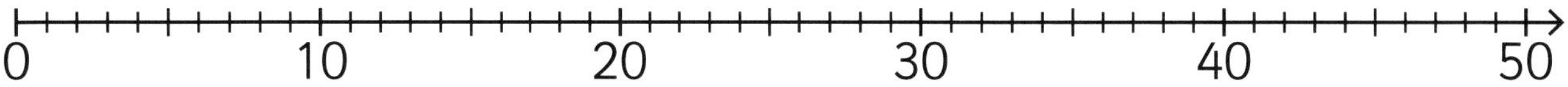

17 24 29 35 42

2. Write the numbers each arrow points to.

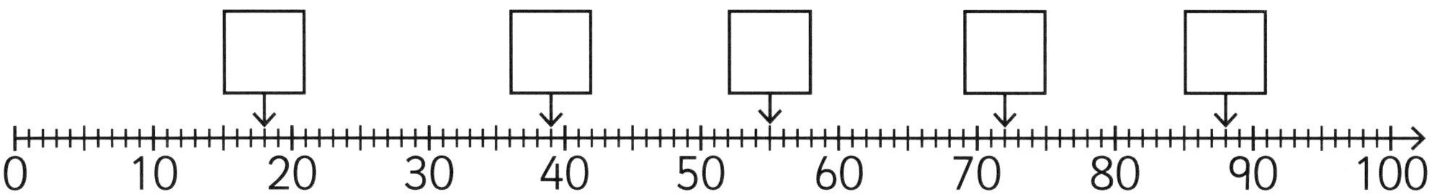

3. Sort these numbers into the circles.

56 81 47 38 64 17 68 28 54 92 59 74

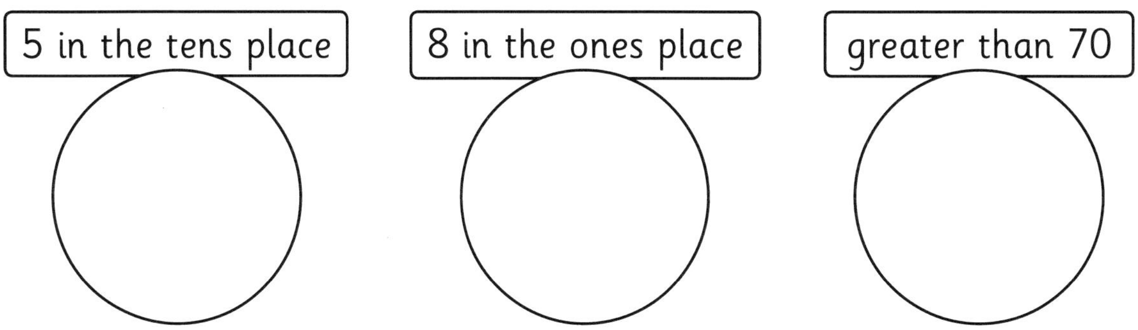

Which numbers are left? ______________________________

Number lines

Your child will use number lines like this at school:

It is a good idea to have one displayed in your home somewhere. Talk about the numbers, comparing them with each other, so that your child can get a good understanding of the order of numbers and their place value.

6.5 Comparing numbers within 100 (1)

Compare and order numbers to 100

1. Join these to their position on the number line.

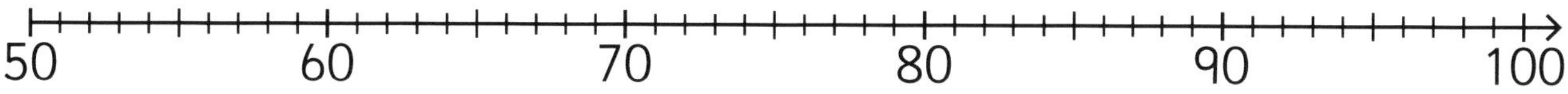

53 67 74 82 95

2. Write the numbers each arrow points to.

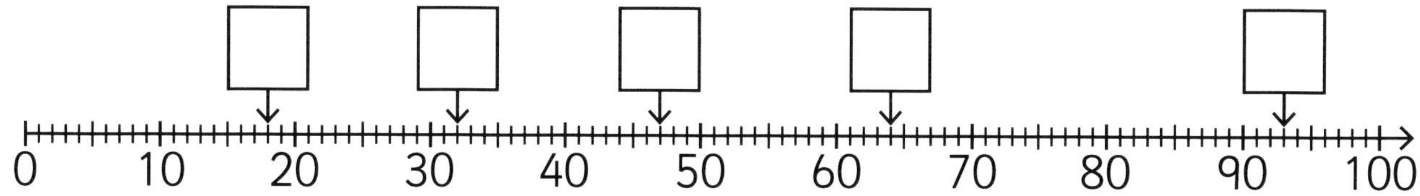

3. Write the numbers in the correct boxes to make each sentence true.

a) 34 45

$\square > \square$

b) 19 26

$\square > \square$

c) 52 63

$\square > \square$

d) 41 14

$\square < \square$

e) 83 86

$\square < \square$

f) 72 91

$\square < \square$

Higher or lower

Play a game of 'Higher or lower' with a set of 20 cards randomly numbered between 1 and 50. Shuffle and place them in a pile face down. Turn over the first card and take turns to predict whether the next card in the pile will be higher or lower. If you are correct you keep the card, if not return the card to the bottom of the pile. Continue until there is only one card left. The player with the most cards is the winner.

6.6 Comparing numbers within 100 (2)

Position, compare and order numbers to 100

1. Write the number that comes before each number.

(a) □ → 38 (b) □ → 56

(c) □ → 41 (d) □ → 65

2. Write the tens number that comes after each number.

(a) 51 → □ (b) 73 → □

(c) 67 → □ (d) 84 → □

3. Fill in the ◯ with < or >.

(a) 38 ◯ 46 (b) 52 ◯ 25

(c) 75 ◯ 7 tens and 2 ones (d) 71 ◯ 39

(e) 9 tens and 3 ones ◯ 97 (f) 56 ◯ 65

4. Write each set in order. Start with the smallest number.

(a) 18, 27, 26, 30, 34

□ □ □ □ □

(b) 52, 61, 45, 72, 59

□ □ □ □ □

Put in order

Use the cards you made for the 'Higher or lower' game. Lay the 20 cards face down and ask your child to pick any four cards and put them in order. If they are correct they keep the cards and continue until all the cards are taken.

6.7 Practice and exercise (I)

Compare and partition 2-digit numbers

1. Write the numbers that come before and after each number.

(a) ☐ → 26 → ☐ (b) ☐ → 45 → ☐ (c) ☐ → 52 → ☐

(d) ☐ → 39 → ☐ (e) ☐ → 68 → ☐ (f) ☐ → 91 → ☐

2. Write the tens numbers that come before and after each number.

(a) ☐ → 54 → ☐ (b) ☐ → 39 → ☐ (c) ☐ → 27 → ☐

(d) ☐ → 21 → ☐ (e) ☐ → 66 → ☐ (f) ☐ → 83 → ☐

3. Write the missing numbers.

(a) 43 – ☐ = 40 (e) 56 – ☐ = 50 (i) 83 – ☐ = 80

(b) 44 – ☐ = 40 (f) 63 – ☐ = 60 (j) 67 – ☐ = 60

(c) 45 – ☐ = 40 (g) 75 – ☐ = 70 (k) 42 – ☐ = 40

(d) 46 – ☐ = 40 (h) 89 – ☐ = 80 (l) 28 – ☐ = 20

4. Add these.

(a) 17 + 3 = ☐ (d) 45 + 5 = ☐ (g) 64 + 6 = ☐

(b) 27 + 3 = ☐ (e) 55 + 5 = ☐ (h) 54 + 6 = ☐

(c) 37 + 3 = ☐ (f) 65 + 5 = ☐ (i) 44 + 6 = ☐

Page numbers

Ask your child to look at page numbers in books, magazines and newspapers. For any page, ask: *How many tens are in this number, and how many ones?* Starting with any page, ask your child what the next two page numbers will be and the two previous page numbers. Now start on any left-hand page and predict what the number on the next left-hand page will be. What about the previous left-hand page?

6.8 Knowing money (1)

Recognise, describe and compare quantities of money

1. Write the value of these coins.

(a) (b) (c) (d) (e) (f) (g) (h)

(a) ☐p (b) ☐p (c) ☐p (d) ☐p (e) ☐p (f) ☐p (g) £☐ (h) £☐

2. Circle the odd one out in each set.

(a)

(b)

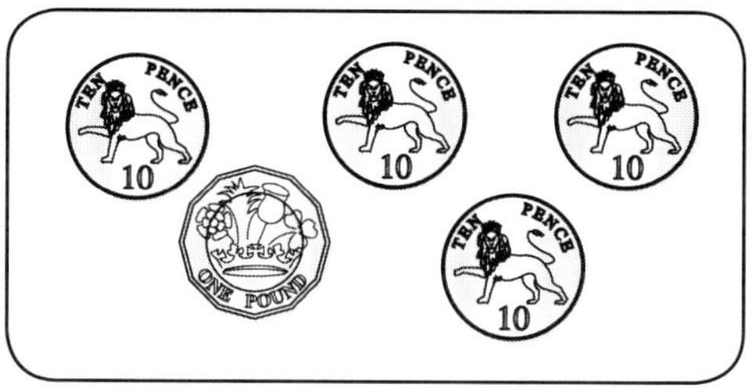

3. Draw these coins in order. Start with the least in value.

a)

b)

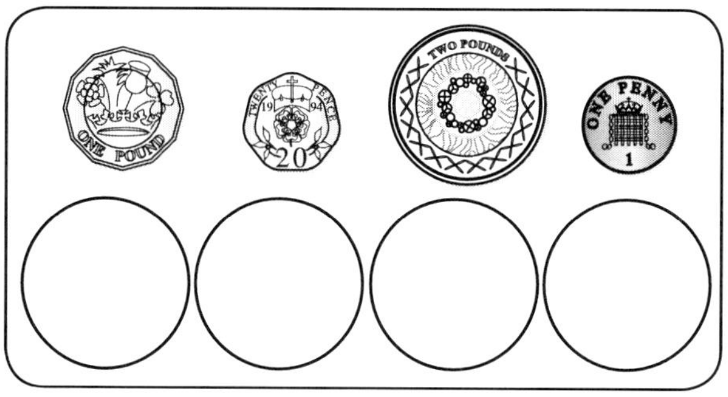

4. Write the value of these notes. Tick the note with the highest value.

(a) £☐ (b) £☐ (c) £☐ (d) £☐

Looking at coins

Gather a handful of different coins and look at them very carefully with your child. Compare how the numbers are written to show each value and talk about the pictures on the coins. Show that some coins with the same value can look different from each other. Draw around or trace the coins to show the shape of each coin always stays the same.

You will need:
coins in a variety of denominations.

6.9 Knowing money (2)

Recognise, describe and compare quantities of money

1. Complete each of these.

a) One  can be exchanged for .

b) One  can be exchanged for .

c) One  can be exchanged for .

d) One  can be exchanged for .

2. Add up the value of these to find the totals.

a)

p

b)

p

c)

£

3. Make 20p in three different ways.

Use 3 coins	Use 4 coins	Use 5 coins

Make 50p

Ask your child to use a pile of 1p, 2p, 5p, 10p and 20p coins to make 50p in different ways. Put the different combinations on a table and compare the groups. Which group has the most coins? Are there any groups with the same number of coins?

You will need:
1p, 2p, 5p, 10p and 20p coins.

7.1 Year, month and day

Recognise and use language relating to days, weeks, months and years

1. Join these days in order. Start with Monday.

Saturday

Sunday

Friday

Monday

Thursday

Wednesday

Tuesday

2. Complete the names of the months for each season.

Spring	Summer	Autumn	Winter
M _ _ c h	J _ _ e	S e _ _ _ _ _ e r	D e _ _ _ _ e r
A _ r i _	_ _ _ l y	O _ _ o b _ _	J _ _ _ _ r y
_ _ y	A _ _ u s _	_ _ v e m _ _ _	_ e b r _ _ _ _

3. Complete these time facts.

(a) ☐ days in a week

(b) ☐ months in a year

(c) ☐ seasons in a year

(d) ☐ days in a weekend

Using a calendar

Make it an everyday event to look at days of the week, the month and the season. Use a paper or e-calendar with your child and encourage them to know the order of the days and months.

7.2 Telling the time

Read the time to the hour and half past the hour

1. Complete the times for each clock.

(a)

o'clock

(b)

half past

(c)

o'clock

(d)

half past

(e)

o'clock

(f)

half past

2. Draw the times on the clocks.

a) 8 o'clock

b) 12 o'clock

c) 3 o'clock

d) 6 o'clock

What's the time Mr Wolf?

The old favourite 'What's the time Mr Wolf?' is still loved by children. Start off as the wolf, with your child asking the time, and give times to the hour in order with your back to your child. Your child takes a step forward for each hour, until you say *Dinner time!* turn around and chase them. It works well to have a 'home' or base such as a chair that your child can try to reach before you catch them.

7.3 Hour and half an hour

Read the time to the hour and half past the hour

1. Write the time for each clock.

(a) 

☐ o'clock

(b) 

half past ☐

(c) 

☐ o'clock

(d) 

half past ☐

2. Draw a line to match the times.

(a) 12:30 (b) 04:30 (c) 07:30

(d) 09:30 (e) 08:00 (f) 11:30

3. These are the start and finish times for a film.

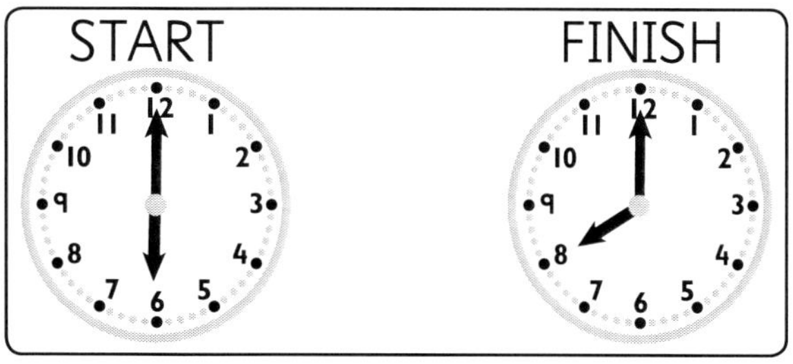

How long does the film last? ☐ hours

Analogue and digital time

It is likely that your child will see digital times more than analogue circular clock-faces. Show your child that the number before the dots is the o'clock that has passed and then show this time on an analogue clock. The minutes, shown after the dots, are the number of minutes that have passed since that 'o'clock'. Your child should understand that when 60 minutes have passed, that will be a whole hour and it will be the next 'o'clock' time.

8.1 Left and right (1)

Recognise and use left and right to describe position and direction

1. Look at these pictures. Colour the left shoes red.
Colour the right gloves blue.

2. Here are the front doors of five houses next door to each other.

(a) House number ☐ is on the left of house number 10.

(b) House number 13 is on the right of house number ☐.

(c) House number 10 is on the ☐ of house number 11.

(d) House number 12 is on the ☐ of house number 11.

Left and right

Play some speed games with your child to see how fast they can respond to left / right instructions, such as: *Touch your left ear*; *Lift your right foot*; *Close your left eye*; *Wave your right hand*; *Touch your right ear with your left hand*.

8.2 Left and right (2)

Recognise and use left and right to describe position and direction

1. Read the instructions and draw a line to put each item on the shelf.

(a) The  is on the right of the .

(b) On the left of the  is the .

(c) The  is on the right of the .

(d) On the right of the  is the .

2. Look at the grid and answer the questions.

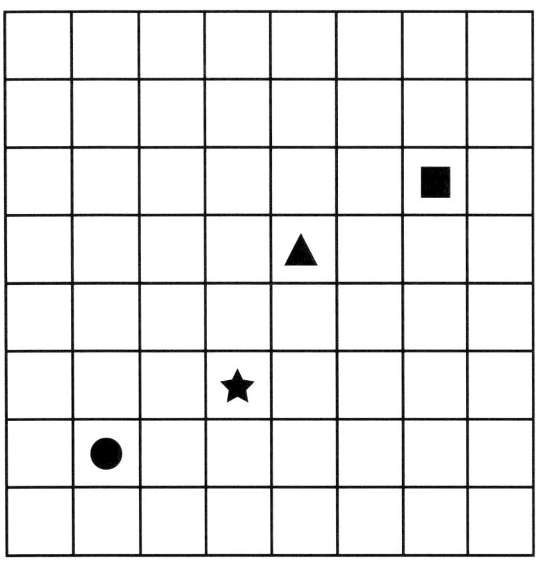

(a) Start from ▲. Move 4 squares left. Move 1 square up. Draw a △.

(b) Start from ■. Move 3 squares down. Move two squares left. Draw a □.

(c) Start from ●. Move 5 squares right. Move 2 squares up. Draw a ○.

(d) Start from ★. Move 2 squares down. Move 4 squares right. Draw a ☆.

Sorting shelves

Take the opportunity to have a tidy up of shelves and drawers with your child. Give instructions as you put things in place, for example: *Put the shoes to the left of the wellies.*

8.3 Left, centre and right and top, middle and bottom

Solve position and movement problems on grids

1. Look at the picture.

Use these words to compete each sentence.

left bottom centre below top above right middle

(a)  is ____________ 

(b)  is on the ____________ row

(c)  is to the ____________ of 

(d)  is in the ____________

(e) 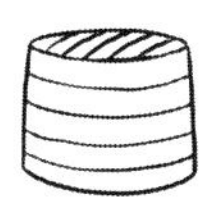 is ____________ 

(f) ,  and  are all in the ____________ row

(g)  is to the ____________ of 

(h) Which word was not used? Make a sentence using that word here.

____

Three in a row

Draw a 3 x 3 grid and use counters in two colours. You have one colour and your child has the other. Take turns to give instructions to the other to place your own counters. For example, you say: *Place a counter in the bottom right square.* Your child then places your counter in the correct place on the grid. The aim of the game is to make a row of three on the grid. You can block each other by placing counters in squares that might make three in a row.

8.4 Comparing lengths

Describe and compare lengths of objects

1. Tick the longest in each group.

(a)

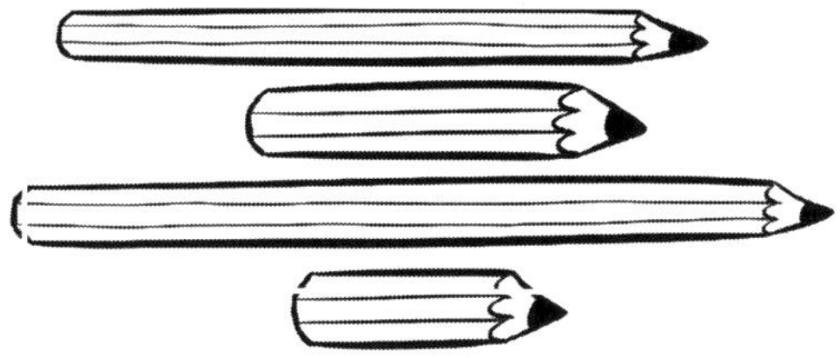

(b)

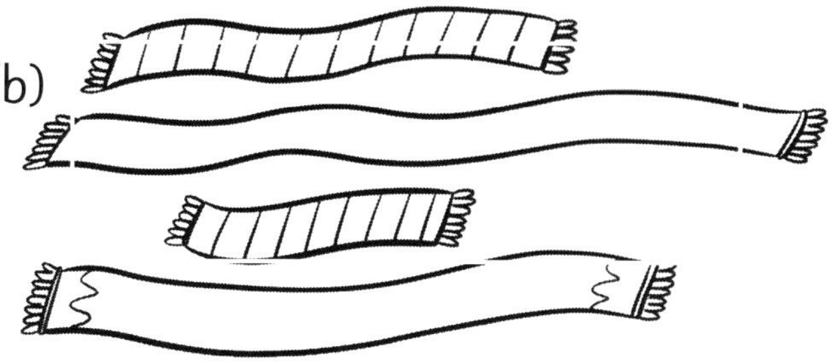

2. Tick the shortest in each group.

(a)

(b)

3. Answer these. Write the number for each tree.

(a) Which tree is the shortest? ☐

(b) Which tree is the tallest? ☐

(c) Which trees are taller than tree 4? ☐ ☐ ☐

(d) Which trees are shorter than tree 1? ☐ ☐ ☐

(e) Write the trees in order starting with the shortest.

☐ ☐ ☐ ☐ ☐

shortest tallest

Comparing fingers

Compare the lengths of your child's fingers to your fingers. Ask them to put their hands together on your hands, palm to palm. Ask: *Who has the longest fingers? Who has shorter fingers? Which is the longest finger? Are any the same length?*

8.5 Length and height (1)

Measure and record lengths

1. Write the length of each of these.

(a) 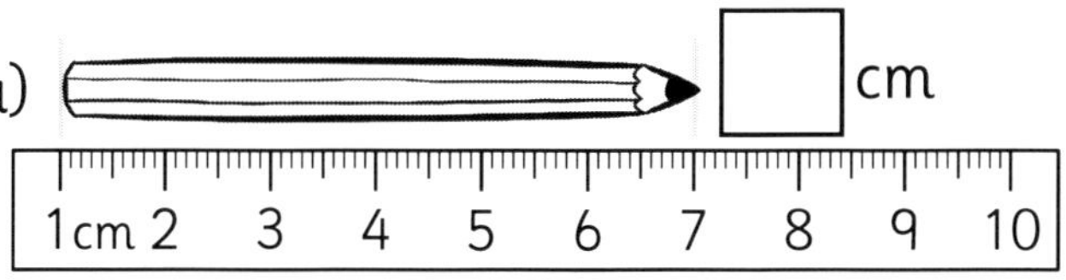

☐ cm

(b) 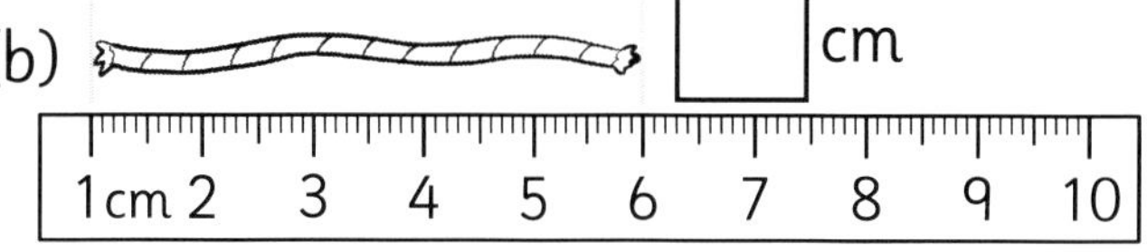

☐ cm

(c) 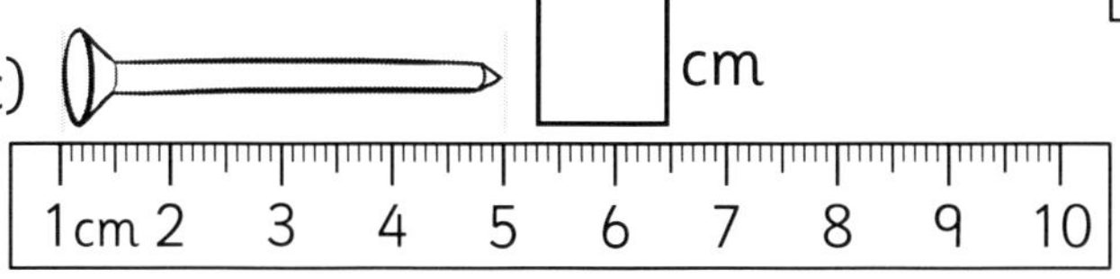

☐ cm

(d) 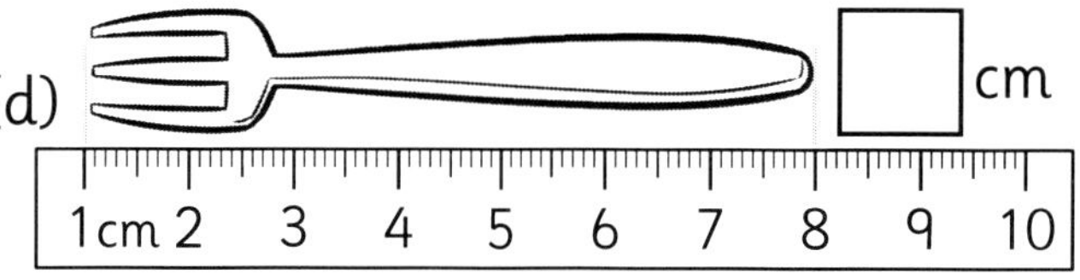

☐ cm

2. Use a ruler to measure the length of each of these.

(a) 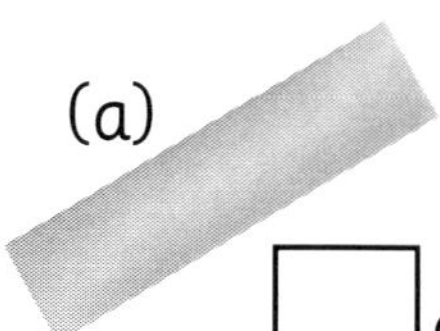

☐ cm

(b) 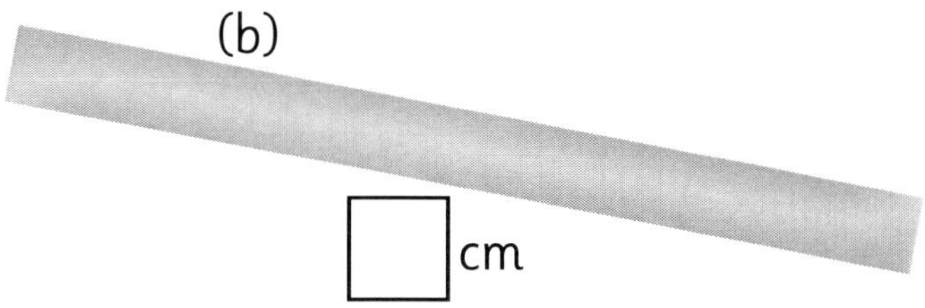

☐ cm

(c) 

☐ cm

(d) 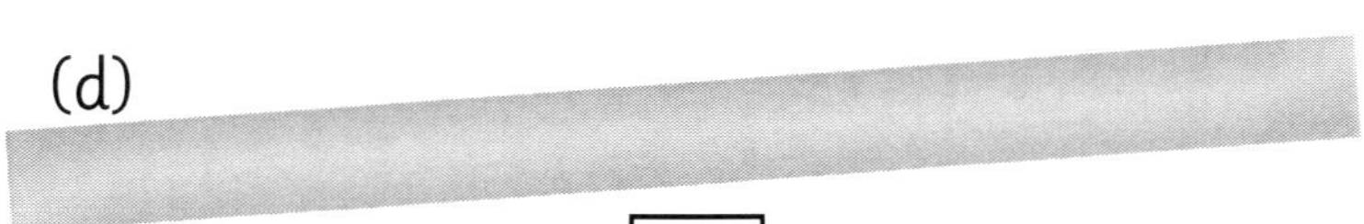

☐ cm

(e) 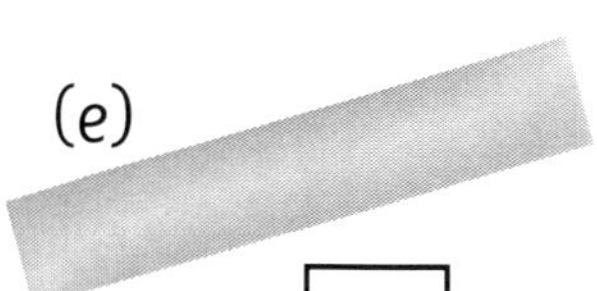

☐ cm

Using a ruler

While using a ruler, emphasise to your child how important it is to line up one end of the item being measured to the zero mark on the ruler, so that it is an accurate measure. Use a simple ruler with only centimetres (no millimetres) marked to begin with and ask your child to find the length of different strips of cards (pre-cut these to exact centimetre lengths 0–15cm). Your child can then lay the strips of paper in order of length.

You will need:
a ruler, strips of card cut to exact centimetre lengths.

8.6 Length and height (2)

Measure and record lengths

1. Use a ruler to measure these lengths.

(a) The toy car has driven ☐ cm. It is ☐ cm to the end.

It will drive a total of ☐ cm.

(b) The toy car has driven ☐ cm. It is ☐ cm to the end.

It will drive a total of ☐ cm.

2. Measure and complete this.

(a) This wool is ☐ cm long.

(b) If 4 cm is cut off, the piece that is left will be ☐ cm long.

3. Write the missing lengths.

(a)

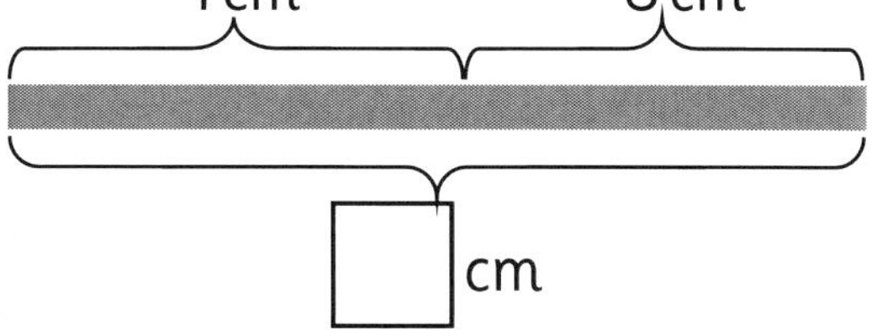

(b)

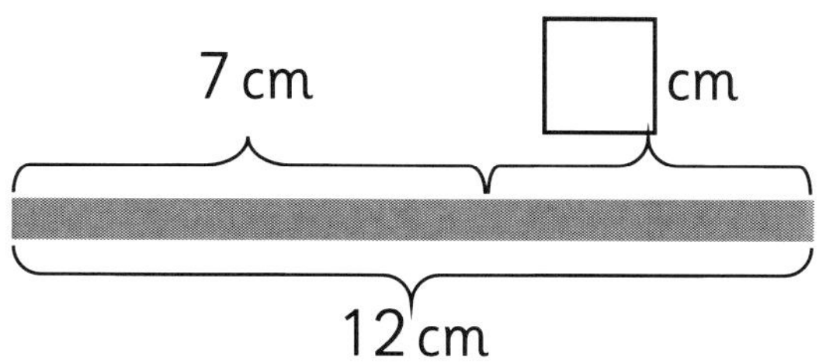

Body measures

Ask your child to use a ruler to measure different parts of their body, for example: finger length, hand span, width of thumb, length of foot.

8.7 Practice and exercise (II)

Describe and compare different quantities of length and time

1. Draw a line from each spot to the length given. Use a ruler to measure and make a straight line.

(a) 6 cm ●

(b) 3 cm ●

(c) 10 cm ●

2. This is part of a longer ruler. Write the length each arrow is pointing to.

(a) ☐ cm (b) ☐ cm (c) ☐ cm (d) ☐ cm (e) ☐ cm

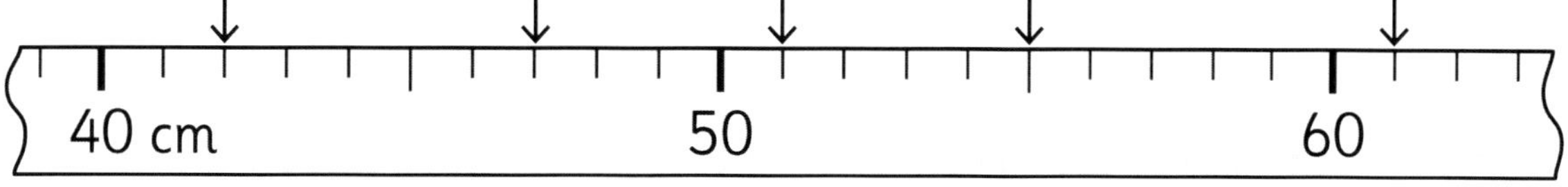

3. Write the times or draw the hands on the clocks to complete each of these.

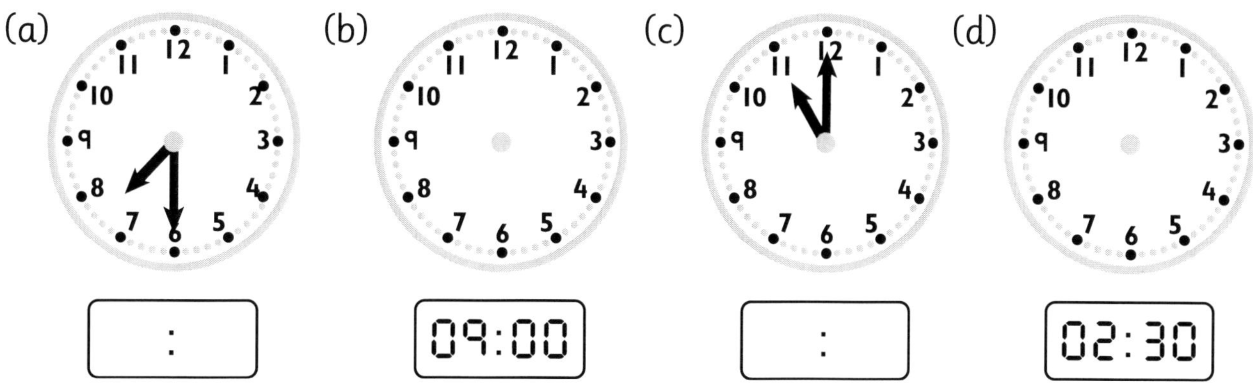

Baking and measuring

Take advantage of opportunities to measure length, weight, capacity and time when cooking with your child. Keep amounts simple so your child can use their measuring skills. For example, they could roll cheese straw pastry to 10 cm long and 2 cm wide and cook for 20 minutes.

Answers

1.1 Let's begin

Q1 bat – ball
key – lock
bowl – spoon
scarf – hat
toothbrush – toothpaste

Q2 5 leaves
6 caterpillars
7 ants
8 sweets

1.2 Let's sort (1)

Q1 4 fan shaped shells and 4 spiral shaped shells

Q2 bird
eraser
apple
triangle

1.3 Let's sort (2)

Q1 4 pears, 5 oranges
3 pens, 6 pencils
4 cars, 3 trains
5 caps, 5 woolly hats

Q2 Possible sets include: 4 with hats; 3 without hats; 3 with shoes; 4 without shoes; 3 with bows; 4 without bows; 4 sitting down; 3 standing up; 2 without eyebrows; 5 with eyebrows; 2 standing on one leg.

1.4 Let's count (1)

Q1 1 rocket, 2 astronauts, 3 moon buggies, 4 space shuttles, 5 shooting stars, 6 suns, 7 planets, 8 rocks, 9 helmets, 10 stars

Q2 one 1, two 2, three 3, four 4, five 5, six 6, seven 7, eight 8, nine 9, ten 10

1.5 Let's count (2)

Q1 5 ants, 4 flowers, 8 fish, 10 footballs, 7 astronauts, 9 rockets

Q2 nine 9, seven 7, eight 8, ten 10

1.6 Let's count (3)

Q1 4 cubes, 2 cuboids, 5 pyramids, 6 spheres, 3 cylinders

Q2 4 squares, 6 rectangles, 8 circles

1.7 Let's count (4)

Q1 2 spots, 4 spots, 6 spots, 8 spots, 10 spots

Q2 3 groups of 5 chickens

Q3 All except extreme left and extreme right.

1.8 Let's count (5)

Q1 own answers

Q2 7, 6, 9, 5, 0, 10

Q3 6 apples, 0 apples, 10 apples, 9 apples

1.9 Let's count (6)

Q1 **(a)** 4 stars, 2 moons
(b) 4 stars, 3 moons
(c) 5 stars, 3 moons
(d) 3 stars, 2 moons
(e) 4 stars, 5 moons
(f) 5 stars, 5 moons

Q2 4, 6, 8, 5, 0, 7

Q3 extra dots: 2, 4, 6, 2, 4, 6

1.10 Counting and ordering numbers (1)

Q1 There are 6 animals.
The elephant is 3rd in the line.
The rhino is 1st in the line.
The giraffe is 4th in the line.
The lion is 2nd in the line.
The zebra is 5th in the line.
The monkey is 6th in the line.

Q2 Colour two rectangles
Colour the second rectangle from the left.
Colour three triangles
Colour the third triangle from the left.
Colour four circles
Colour the fourth circle from the left.
Colour five squares
Colour the fifth square from the left.

1.11 Counting and ordering numbers (2)

Q1 2nd down Second 2nd
3rd down Third 3rd
6th down Fourth 4th
5th down Fifth 5th
top one Sixth 6th

Q2 1st getting out of bed
2nd getting dressed
3rd having breakfast
4th going to school

1.12 Let's compare (1)

Q1 **(a)** top line
(b) bottom line

Q2 3rd set

Q3 any from: 5 balls, 1 fewer; 4 balls, 2 fewer; 3 balls, 3 fewer; 2 balls, 4 fewer; 1 ball, 5 fewer

1.13 Let's compare (2)

Q1 $5 > 4$, $3 < 5$, $6 = 6$, $6 > 5$

Q2 $5 > 3$, $4 = 4$, $4 < 5$

Q3 any number less than 6, any number less than 10, any number greater than 8, any number greater than 2
any number greater than 4, any number greater than 7, any number less than 5, any number less than 9

1.14 The number line

Q1 own answers

Q2 **(a)** 2, 4, 5
(b) 7, 8, 9
(c) 1, 4, 5
(d) 3, 4, 7

Q3 3, 5, 6, 9, 10

2.1 Number bonds

Q1 5, 4, 3, 2

Q2 3, 3, 5
5, 3, 7

2.2 Addition (1)

Q1 **(a)** $2 + 3 = 5$, $3 + 2 = 5$
(b) $4 + 3 = 7$, $3 + 4 = 7$
(c) $4 + 5 = 9$, $5 + 4 = 9$
(d) $6 + 4 = 10$, $4 + 6 = 10$

Q2 = 5: 3 + 2, 1 + 4, 2 + 3, 4 + 1
= 6: 1 + 5, 2 + 4, 3 + 3, 4 + 2

2.3 Addition (2)

Q1 (a) 10
(b) 9
(c) 8
(d) 3 + 7 = 10
(e) 4 + 6 = 10
(f) 5 + 5 = 10

Q2 (a)–(f) any from: 1 + 7, 2 + 6, 3 + 5, 4 + 4, 5 + 3, 6 + 2, 7 + 1

Q3 (a) 5
(b) 9
(c) 7
(d) 6
(e) 6
(f) 9

2.4 Addition (3)

Q1 (a) 2 + 3 = 5
(b) 3 + 4 = 7
(c) 5 + 2 = 7
(d) 4 + 4 = 8

Q2 (a) 4 + 2 = 6
(b) 6 + 2 = 8
(c) 7 + 2 = 9

Q3 (a) 5
(b) 9
(c) 6
(d) 6
(e) 5
(f) 9

2.5 Let's talk and calculate (I)

Q1 (a) 2 + 3 = 5
(b) 4 + 2 = 6
(c) 5 + 3 = 8
(d) 4 + 4 = 8

Q2 (a) 3 + 2 = 5
(b) 4 + 5 = 9
(c) 6 + 3 = 9
(d) 2 + 1 = 3
(e) 6 + 2 = 8
(f) 5 + 5 = 10
(g) 2 + 2 = 4
(h) 8 + 1 = 9
(i) 4 + 3 = 7

2.6 Subtraction (1)

Q1 (a) 4 subtract 1 is 3, 4 – 1 = 3
(b) 8 subtract 3 is 5, 8 – 3 = 5
(c) 6 subtract 2 is 4, 6 – 2 = 4
(d) 8 subtract 2 is 6, 8 – 2 = 6

Q2 (a) 5 – 1 = 4
(b) 5 – 2 = 3
(c) 5 – 3 = 2
(d) 6 – 4 = 2
(e) 6 – 3 = 3
(f) 6 – 2 = 4

2.7 Subtraction (2)

Q1 (a) 2, 6 – 4 = 2
(b) 5, 8 – 3 = 5
(c) 4, 9 – 5 = 4
(d) 5, 7 – 2 = 5

Q2 (a) 2
(b) 1
(c) 2
(d) 2
(e) 1
(f) 2
(g) 2
(h) 3
(i) 6

2.8 Subtraction (3)

Q1 (a) 3
(b) 4
(c) 5
(d) 3
(e) 4
(f) 3

Q2 (a) 7 – 5 = 2
(b) 8 – 2 = 6
(c) 9 – 4 = 5
(d) 10 – 6 = 4

2.9 Let's talk and calculate (II)

Q1 (a) 5 – 2 = 3
(b) 6 – 2 = 4
(c) 8 – 3 = 5
(d) 7 – 5 = 2

Q2 (a) 4
(b) 5
(c) 3
(d) 3
(e) 5
(f) 7
(g) 4
(h) 5
(i) 6

Q3 (a) 0
(b) 1
(c) 3
(d) 3
(e) 3
(f) 7

2.10 Addition and subtraction

Q1 (a) 6 + 2 = 8
(b) 8 – 2 = 6
(c) 7 + 2 = 9
(d) 9 – 2 = 7

Q2 (a) 5
(b) 9
(c) 3, 3
(d) 4, 8

2.11 Addition and subtraction using a number line

Q1 (a) 2 + 4 = 6
(b) 8 – 5 = 3

Q2 (a) arrow from 6 to 10, 6 + 4 = 10
(b) arrow from 9 to 3, 9 – 6 = 3

2.12 Games of number 10

Q1 (a) 3
(b) 2
(c) 5
(d) 4

Q2 0 → 10, 1 → 9, 2 → 8, 3 → 7, 4 → 6, 5 → 5

Q3 (a) 5
(b) 4
(c) 10
(d) 9
(e) 9

2.13 Adding three numbers

Q1 (a) 5 + 1 + 3 = 9
(b) 3 + 3 + 3 = 9

Q2 1 + 3 + 3 = 7

Q3 (a) 7
(b) 9
(c) 9
(d) 9
(e) 10
(f) 8

2.14 Subtracting three numbers

Q1 (a) 4
(b) 10 − 5 − 2 = 3

Q2 8 − 3 − 3 = 2

Q3 (a) 2
(b) 3
(c) 3
(d) 1
(e) 1
(f) 0

2.15 Mixed addition and subtraction

Q1 (a) 3 + 5 − 3 = 5
(b) 9 − 5 + 3 = 7

Q2 (a) >
(b) =
(c) =
(d) <

3.1 Numbers 11–20

Q1 top row: 4, 6, 8, 9
bottom row: 12, 13, 16, 17, 18, 20

Q2 (a) 14
(b) 14
(c) 16

Q3 (a) 16, 12, 10, 6, 2
(b) 17, 11, 7, 5, 1

Q4 (a) 17
(b) 12, 15
(c) own answers

3.2 Tens and ones

Q1 (a) 16
(b) 15
(c) 18
(d) 19

Q2 (a) 14
(b) 17
(c) 10 + 6 = 16
(d) 10 + 3 = 13

Q3 (a) 5, 9, 7
(b) 14, 11, 3
(c) 10, 10, 10

3.3 Ordering numbers up to 20

Q1 9 → 10 → 11 → 12 → 13 → 14 → 15 → 16 → 17→ 18 → 19 → 20

Q2 (a) 18 and 17, 14, 15, 16, 17, 18, 19, 20
(b) 13 and 11, 8, 9, 10, 11, 12, 13, 14

3.4 Addition and subtraction (1)

Q1 (a) 8, 18
(b) 1, 11

Q2 (a) 9, 19
(b) 5, 5
(c) 5, 15
(d) 4, 14
(e) 5, 5
(f) 9, 19

3.5 Addition and subtraction (II) (1)

Q1 (a) 11
(b) 12
(c) 13
(d) 14

Q2 (a) 3, 13
(b) 2, 4, 14
(c) 1, 3, 13
(d) 3, 2, 12

3.6 Addition and subtraction (II) (2)

Q1 (a) 5 + 6 = 11 6 + 5 = 11
(b) 8 + 6 = 14 6 + 8 = 14
(c) 14 = 9 + 5 14 = 5 + 9
(d) 15 = 8 + 7 15 = 7 + 8

Q2 (a) >
(b) =
(c) <
(d) >
(e) >
(f) =

3.7 Addition and subtraction (II) (3)

Q1 (a) 8
(b) 6
(c) 8
(d) 9

Q2 (a) 1, 9
(b) 2, 5, 5
(c) 4, 4, 6
(d) 3, 2, 8
(e) 7, 1, 9
(f) 6, 3, 7

3.8 Addition and subtraction (II) (4)

Q1 (a) 11 − 3 = 8
(b) 14 − 5 = 9
(c) 12 − 4 = 8
(d) 12 − 6 = 6

Q2 Difference 5, 4, 5, 5, 7, 7

3.9 Addition and subtraction (II) (5)

Q1 (a) 6 + 6 = 12
(b) 7 + 5 = 12

Q2 (c), (f) = 7
(b), (g) = 9
(d), (e) = 11
(a), (h) = 13

3.10 Let's talk and calculate (III)

Q1 (a) 5 + 6 = 11
(b) 12 − 3 = 9

Q2 (a) 3
(b) 4

3.11 Adding on and taking away

Q1 (a) 5 + 9 = 14, 14 − 9 = 5
(b) 6 + 7 = 13, 13 − 7 = 6

Q2 (a) 13
(b) 15, 3
(c) 5, 5
(d) 7, 7

3.12 Number walls

Q1 (a) example
(b) middle row 9, 5
top row 14
(c) bottom row 4
middle row 11
top row 21
(d) bottom row 5, 3
middle row 8
(e) bottom row 3
middle row 10
top row 19
(f) bottom row 7, 1
middle row 10

Q2 (a) row 3 4, 3, 4
row 2 7, 7
row 1 14
(b) row 4 3, 2
row 3 7, 3
row 2 12

Q3 (a), (b) Own answers, check each is different

4.1 Shapes of objects (1)

Q1 (a) ball
(b) food can
(c) ice cream cone
(d) dice
(e) tea caddy
(f) pyramid

Q2 (a) 1
(b) 3
(c) 4
(d) 3
(e) 6

4.2 Shapes of objects (2)

Q1 (a) cylinder
(b) pyramid
(c) sphere
(d) cube
(e) cone

Q2 circular lids → correct sized cylinders
square lid → cube
rectangular lids → correct sized cuboids

5.1 Sorting shapes

Q1 (a) 7 circles
(b) 4 squares
(c) 10 rectangles

Q2 Check each shape is joined to the correct section on the table. There are 2 triangles.

5.2 Calculating with reasoning

Q1 (a) 17
(b) 16
(c) 15
(d) 14
(e) 13
(f) 11
(g) 12
(h) 13
(i) 14
(j) 15
(k) 15
(l) 16
(m) 17
(n) 18
(o) 19

Q2 (a) 10
(b) 9
(c) 8
(d) 10
(e) 9
(f) 8
(g) 7
(h) 7
(i) 7

Q3 (a) 14 – 6
(b) 5 + 9

5.3 Comparing numbers

Q1 (a) 10 squares
(b) 6 circles

Q2 (a) >
(b) <
(c) <
(d) =
(e) >
(f) >
(g) <
(h) >
(i) <

5.4 Half and quarter

Q1 (a) (b) (d)

Q2 Check pupils' answers.

Q3 (a) 4 + 4 = 8
(b) 5 + 5 = 10
(c) 6 + 6 = 12

Q4 (a) 12
(b) 7
(c) 8
(d) 18

5.5 Let's do additions together

Q1 (a) 5 + 6 8 + 3
(b) 8 + 5 4 + 9
(c) 7 + 8 6 + 9
(d) 7 + 10 9 + 8

Q2 (a) example
(b) 9
(c) 8
(d) 7
(e) 6
(f) 4
(g) 5
(h) 6 + 8
(i) 7 + 7
(j) 8 + 6
(k) 10
(l) 9
(m) 8 + 8
(n) 9 + 7
(o) 10 + 6

5.6 Let's do subtraction together

Q1 (a) 11 – 8, 12 – 9
(b) 9 – 5, 13 – 9
(c) 12 – 7, 14 – 9
(d) 15 – 9, 9 – 3

Q2 (a) example
(b) 9
(c) 8
(d) 7
(e) 6
(f) 11
(g) 12
(h) 13 – 5
(i) 14 – 6
(j) 15 – 7
(k) 1
(l) 2
(m) 12 – 3
(n) 13 – 4
(o) 14 – 5

Q3 14 – 8 = 6

5.7 Making number sentences

Q1 (a) 6 + 3 = 9
(b) 3 + 6 = 9
(c) 9 − 3 = 6
(d) 9 − 6 = 3

Q2 (a) 8 + 6 = 14, 6 + 8 = 14, 14 − 6 = 8, 14 − 8 = 6
(b) 7 + 5 = 12, 5 + 7 = 12, 12 − 5 = 7, 12 − 7 = 5

5.8 Mathematics playground (1)

Q1 (a) 12, 13, 15, 16, 18
(b) 10, 12, 16, 18
(c) 5, 9, 15, 17

Q2 (a) <
(b) >
(c) =
(d) =
(e) >
(f) >
(g) <
(h) =
(i) >

Q3 (a) 6 + 8 = 14
(b) 8 + 6 = 14
(c) 14 − 8 = 6
(d) 14 − 6 = 8

5.9 Mathematics playground (2)

Q1 (a) 4 + 3 = 6 + 1, 9 − 2 = 11 − 4, 5 + 2 = 15 − 8
(b) 4 + 5 = 11 − 2, 15 − 6 = 3 + 6, 0 + 9 = 13 − 4

Q2 (a) 9 + 4 = 13
(b) 13 − 4 = 9
(c) 13 − 9 = 4
(d) 5 + 8 = 13
(e) 13 − 5 = 8
(f) 13 − 8 = 5
(g) 6 + 7 = 13
(h) 13 − 7 = 6
(i) 13 − 6 = 7

5.10 Mathematics Playground (3)

Q1 top line: 10 + 4, 10 + 5, 10 + 7, 10 + 8, 10 + 9, 10 + 10
bottom line: 12, 13, 16, 17, 18, 19, 20

Q2 (a) 10
(b) 11
(c) 12
(d) 13
(e) 14
(f) 9, 15
(g) 4
(h) 5
(i) 6
(j) 7
(k) 8
(l) 15, 9

6.1 Tens and ones

Q1 (a) 3 tens and 6 ones equals 36, 30 + 6 = 36
(b) 5 tens and 4 ones equals 54, 50 + 4 = 54
(c) 4 tens and 9 ones equals 49, 40 + 9 = 49
(d) 6 tens and 2 ones equals 62, 60 + 2 = 62

Q2 (a) 34
(b) 56
(c) 43
(d) 65

6.2 Knowing 100

Q1 20, 40, 50, 60, 80, 90, 100

Q2 (a) 60
(b) 70
(c) 80
(d) 90
(e) 100
(f) 30
(g) 30
(h) 30
(i) 30
(j) 30
(k) 10
(l) 20
(m) 30
(n) 40
(o) 50
(p) 40
(q) 50
(r) 60
(s) 70
(t) 80

6.3 Repeating numbers up to 100 (1)

Q1 (a) 6 tens and 2 ones equals 62
(b) 7 tens and 3 ones equals 73
(c) 8 tens and 6 ones equals 86
(d) 5 tens and 9 ones equals 59

Q2 (a) 3 tens and 4 ones, 34
(b) 5 tens and 6 ones, 56
(c) 4 tens and 7 ones, 47
(d) 6 tens and 5 ones, 65

6.4 Representing numbers up to 100 (2)

Q1 Lines drawn from 17, 24, 29, 35, 42 to number line.

Q2 18, 39, 55, 72, 88

Q3 5 tens: 56, 54, 59
8 ones: 38, 68, 28
greater than 70: 81, 92, 74
numbers left: 47, 64, 17

6.5 Comparing numbers within 100 (1)

Q1 Lines drawn from 53, 67, 74, 82, 95 to number line.

Q2 18, 32, 47, 64, 93

Q3 (a) 45 > 34
(b) 26 > 19
(c) 63 > 52
(d) 14 < 41
(e) 83 < 86
(f) 72 < 91

6.6 Comparing numbers within 100 (2)

Q1 (a) 37
(b) 55
(c) 40
(d) 64

Q2 (a) 61
(b) 83
(c) 77
(d) 94

Q3 (a) <
(b) >
(c) >
(d) >
(e) <
(f) <

Q4 (a) 18, 26, 27, 30, 34
(b) 45, 52, 59, 61, 72

6.7 Practice and exercise (I)

Q1 (a) 25, 27
(b) 44, 46
(c) 51, 53
(d) 38, 40
(e) 67, 69
(f) 90, 92

Q2 (a) 44, 64
(b) 29, 49
(c) 17, 37
(d) 11, 31
(e) 56, 76
(f) 73, 93

Q3 (a) 3
(b) 4
(c) 5
(d) 6
(e) 6
(f) 3
(g) 5
(h) 9
(i) 3
(j) 7
(k) 2
(l) 8

Q4 (a) 20
(b) 30
(c) 40
(d) 50
(e) 60
(f) 70
(g) 70
(h) 60
(i) 50

6.8 Knowing Money (1)

Q1 (a) 1p
(b) 2p
(c) 5p
(d) 10p
(e) 20p
(f) 50p
(g) £1
(h) £2

Q2 (a) 5p
(b) £1

Q3 (a) 2p, 5p, 10p, 50p
(b) 1p, 20p, £1, £2

Q4 (a) £20
(b) £50 ✓
(c) £10
(d) £5

6.9 Knowing money (2)

Q1 (a) 2
(b) 4
(c) 2
(d) 5

Q2 (a) 35p
(b) 90p
(c) £2

Q3 10p, 5p, 5p
5p, 5p, 5p, 5p
1p, 2p, 2p, 5p, 10p

7.1 Year, month and day

Q1 Monday → Tuesday → Wednesday → Thursday → Friday → Saturday → Sunday

Q2 Spring: March, April, May
Summer: June, July, August
Autumn: September. October, November
Winter: December, January, February

Q3 (a) 7
(b) 12
(c) 4
(d) 2

7.2 Telling the time

Q1 (a) 7 o'clock
(b) half past 2
(c) 10 o'clock
(d) half past 1
(e) 9 o'clock
(f) half past 4

Q2 Check the hands are drawn accurately to show the correct times.

7.3 Hour and half an hour

Q1 (a) 5 o'clock
(b) half past 8
(c) 1 o'clock
(d) half past 11

Q2 Lines drawn to clocks from the left: e, f, d, c, b, a

Q3 2 hours

8.1 Left and right (1)

Q1 All left shoes coloured red. All right gloves coloured blue.

Q2 (a) 9
(b) 12
(c) left
(d) right

8.2 Left and right (2)

Q1 Check objects are in this order from left to right: ball, train, car, book, jigsaw, teddy, racket.

Q2 (a) △ (1,6)
(b) □ (5,3)
(c) ○ (7,4)
(d) ☆ (8,1)

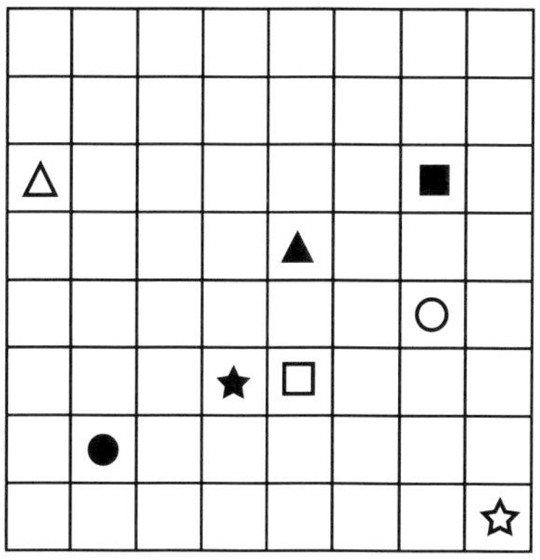

8.3 Left, centre and right and top, middle and bottom

Q1 (a) above
(b) bottom
(c) right
(d) centre
(e) below
(f) middle
(g) left
(h) top

8.4 Comparing lengths

Q1 (a) 3rd pencil
(b) 2nd scarf

Q2 (a) 3rd rock
(b) 3rd shoe

Q3 (a) 5
(b) 3
(c) 1, 2, 3
(d) 2, 4, 5
(e) 5, 4, 2, 1, 3

8.5 Length and height (1)

Q1 (a) 7 cm
(b) 6 cm
(c) 5 cm
(d) 8 cm

Q2 (a) 3 cm
(b) 9 cm
(c) 2 cm
(d) 10 cm
(e) 4 cm

8.6 Length and height (2)

Q1 (a) 4 cm, 5 cm, 9 cm
(b) 6 cm 7 cm, 13 cm

Q2 (a) 9 cm
(b) 5 cm

Q3 (a) 17 cm
(b) 5 cm

8.7 Practice and exercise (II)

Q1 Measure each line to check it is accurate.

Q2 (a) 42 cm
(b) 47 cm
(c) 51 cm
(d) 55 cm
(e) 61 cm

Q3 (a) 07:30
(b) Check time is drawn correctly.
(c) 11:00
(d) Check time is drawn correctly.

Notes

Notes

Notes

Notes

Notes

HarperCollins
PUBLISHERS
Since 1817

William Collins' dream of knowledge for all began with the publication of his first book in 1819.

A self-educated mill worker, he not only enriched millions of lives, but also founded a flourishing publishing house. Today, staying true to this spirit, Collins books are packed with inspiration, innovation and practical expertise. They place you at the centre of a world of possibility and give you exactly what you need to explore it.

Collins. Freedom to teach.

Published by Collins
An imprint of HarperCollins*Publishers*
The News Building
1 London Bridge Street
London
SE1 9GF

Browse the complete Collins catalogue at
www.collins.co.uk

10 9 8 7 6 5 4 3 2

978-0-00-824145-2

Author: Paul Broadbent

Homework Guide Series Editor: Amanda Simpson

Practice Books Series Editor: Professor Lianghuo Fan

British Library Cataloguing in Publication Data

A catalogue record for this publication is available from the British Library.

Publishing Manager: Fiona McGlade
In-house Senior Editor: Mike Appleton
In-house Editorial Assistant: August Stevens
Project Manager: Emily Hooton
Copy Editor: Tracy Thomas
Proofreader: Karen Williams
Answers: Gillian Rich
Cover design: Kevin Robbins and East China Normal University Press Ltd.
Internal design: 2Hoots Publishing Services Ltd
Typesetting: 2Hoots Publishing Services Ltd
Illustrations: QBS
Production: Sarah Burke

Printed and bound by CPI Group (UK) Ltd, Croydon, CR0 4YY